A COMPANION TO THE CATECHISM

A Reader's Guide

Edited by Patrick M. Devitt

VERITAS

First published 1995 by
Veritas Publications
7-8 Lower Abbey Street
Dublin 1

Copyright © The individual contributors, 1995

ISBN 1 85390 224 1

The numbers in parenthesis throughout this volume refer to the paragraphs of the *Catechism of the Catholic Church,* English translation, copyright © (in Ireland) 1994 Veritas Publications – Libreria Editrice Vaticana. All rights reserved. The poem 'A Giving' (pp. 70-71) is published in Brendan Kennelly's *Collected Poems* (Bloodaxe Books, 1981).

Cover design by Banahan McManus
Printed in the Republic of Ireland by Criterion Press Ltd, Dublin

CONTENTS

1. Why a Catechism? 5
   Patrick M. Devitt

2. Scripture in the Catechism of the Catholic Church 17
   Michael Maher

3. I Believe – We Believe
   Faith and Doctrine in the Catechism 27
   Eoin G. Cassidy

4. The Profession of the Christian Faith: the Creeds 39
   Breandán Leahy

5. The Seven Sacraments of the Church 48
   Catherine Gorman

6. Morality and the Catechism 59
   Donal Harrington

7. Prayer in the Catechism 69
   Donal Neary SJ

Appendix – Signposts 78
   Bishop Donal Murray

Notes 83

Notes on Contributors 88

1

WHY A CATECHISM?
Communicating the New Catechism in a Pastoral Setting

Patrick M. Devitt

What the *Catechism of the Catholic Church*[1] is not
Whenever we hear the word 'catechism', many of us automatically think of a book containing questions and answers which were memorised in school by children.[2] However, the CCC is a very different type of book. It is a much more detailed and much more nuanced exposition of the Catholic faith, and it does not use the question and answer technique. The CCC is definitely not intended for children. It is written primarily for bishops in their role as teachers of the faith (12). It gives a systematic presentation of the teaching of the Church, as this has been elaborated over the centuries (18). Its style is expository rather than argumentative. It presents rather than argues its case. In this respect, it differs from the best of contemporary theology which tries, not just to recall the traditional teachings, but even more so to reformulate the substance of the faith in terms of the newly emerging questions of today.

The CCC is not without precedents. It is heir to a long tradition of catechisms (8-9). The first printed catechism was Luther's *Small Catechism*, published in German in 1529. This was subsequently translated into most European languages, and thereby set the tone for many later catechisms. Most of our common assumptions about catechisms derive ultimately from this Reformation document. Since it is a very small book, it is often referred to as a 'minor catechism'. Furthermore, it is in question and answer form, and is meant to be used in the household by the father with his children and his servants. However, when the Council of Trent decided to publish a catechism in response to Luther's, it produced a totally different type of book. It produced a 'major catechism', in size and comprehensive nature the equivalent of the CCC. This catechism (often called the *Roman Catechism*) was not meant for use in households but rather as a reference book for parish priests, who were expected to draw from it in preparing their sermons. Nor was it written in question and answer style but was designed, as is the CCC, to be 'a compendium of all Catholic doctrine' (*FD* 3).[3]

Luther established a certain tradition through the writing of his *Small*

Catechism. Though the *Roman Catechism* opted for another approach, nevertheless, within the later Catholic tradition authors such as Canisius, Bellarmine, Challoner and Butler borrowed instead from Luther's approach and produced a range of Catholic catechisms, in question and answer style, for children of different ages.

'Useful reading for all other Christian faithful' (12)

Though they wrote primarily for bishops, the authors of the CCC also aimed at a far wider readership (*FD* 3). They have not been disappointed. Millions of copies in several languages have been sold already. Clearly many people are interested in what it has to say. Both inside and outside the Catholic family, there is a genuine curiosity about Catholic teaching on many different issues. The CCC invites all interested people to take and read: to enter into a vast supermarket of teachings, seeking first to find a particular offer, but likely later to pick up many other items as well.

One of the greatest needs in the Catholic Church today is to offer all adults a challenge to their faith. Adult catechesis provides people with many different opportunities to continue maturing in the faith all through their lives (4-5, 2688). Already, many small groups of parishioners are forming study circles to read the CCC. Anyone who still thinks that catechisms are meant only for children will be pleasantly surprised by the CCC, which assumes a readership gifted with theological and spiritual sophistication.

Many people still tend to identify religion with morality. When Church teaching is mentioned, they immediately think of what the Church has to say about sexual morality. They are often surprised to realise that the Church, which has a lot to say about sex, also has a lot to say about issues of social justice and honesty and living life to the full. These issues are also treated in the CCC (2401-2513). Sex is not the only item on the Church's moral agenda. Some people are often surprised to realise that the Church has much more to say about God, about Christ, about the Holy Spirit, about the Paschal Mystery, about the seven sacraments, about forms of prayer, than it has to say about sex. If one wanted a comprehensive overview of what the Catholic Church has taught in its long history, a good place to begin would be the CCC. The CCC summarises hundreds of agenda items that have been pondered over and decided upon by the Church during almost two thousand years of meetings and assemblies.

People today often say that they want to believe in God, or even in Jesus Christ, but that the Church leaves them cold. Such people could gain a lot of insight from a study of the CCC. There they will learn that the Church has a profound sense of her own sinfulness (977-80) and sees herself simply as a provisional sacrament of the Trinity (775). What ultimately matters for the Church is not how she is, but how the God she speaks for is being revealed. The greatest insight to be gained from a careful reading of the CCC is a sense of the triune God – Father, Son and Holy Spirit – as the beginning and end of all that was, that is and is yet to be (232-4). For people whose image of God is a Lord Kitchener pointing with outstretched index finger at an unwilling people, and making them feel guilty about all they are not doing for their country, even a very brief reading of the CCC will suggest instead that the finger of God is most accurately imaged by the writing on the sand which Jesus did as he refused to condemn the sinful woman.

One helpful way to read the CCC is to remember that the Christian faith in Ireland is still only fifteen hundred years old. There have been people in Ireland for longer than that. And it is likely that there will be people for thousands or millions of years yet. Inevitably the CCC captures the past more than the present or the future. Furthermore, in its evocation of the past, it has selected some voices more than others. There is absolutely nothing wrong with a book that gives a voice to our dead. Tradition, after all, is the democracy of the dead. All good catechesis wants to give a voice to the dead. But it is also good catechetical practice to give a voice to the many voiceless ones of the past as well as to those many voiceless ones who are alive today. Put in another way, if catechesis is a choir trying to sing in harmony, there are many gaps still in the choir and many singers still to be invited in. This will take a lot of time and energy (2226).

Colm Tóibín's *The Sign of the Cross: Travels in Catholic Europe* is a remarkable book in that it outlines the variety and imaginative richness of Christian religious ritual in Europe. It evokes the period of Christendom when European culture was permeated with Christian symbols. But Catholic Europe is surely more than its rituals. Catholic Europe also includes many universities where the faith is studied in a rigorous manner (158). One looks in vain for any reference by Tóibín to the intellectual achievements of Catholic Europe. It's as if there never was a Rahner, or a de Lubac, or a von Balthasar. It's as if nothing ever happened in the Gregorian or in Tübingen, in Louvain or in Maynooth. The CCC, for all its limitations, is convinced that a serious intellectual articulation of the faith is a worthwhile enterprise (94-5). In this belief it provides a modest complement to the work of novelists and travel writers, by offering an outline syllabus for theological reflection and study. This syllabus, of course, still needs to be fleshed out in works of serious theology, drawing on traditional wisdom to find new faith responses to the questions of today.

Communicating the CCC in a pastoral setting

The back cover of the CCC outlines the main reasons why it was written, namely, to provide a reference text for local catechisms, to become a source of deeper personal knowledge of the faith (429), to be a support for ecumenism, and to give an account of the hope that is in us (*FD* 3).

Later on I shall examine the first of these issues, but here I shall concentrate on the second issue, how the CCC can be a source for deeper knowledge of the faith. I shall explore the image of the faith as a symphony (*FD* 4), within which a wondrous harmony (*FD* 6) is possible. This will require a brief look at the *content* and *structure* of the new *Catechism*. Then I will suggest how to communicate the riches of the CCC in different life contexts. Here I will be examining the *spirit* of the CCC, especially the need for pastoral sensitivity in communicating its contents.

Four pillars of the faith (13)

The CCC falls into four sections, each of which corresponds to a section of the *Roman Catechism*, and each of which could be understood as a response to four fundamental human quests.

Part 1, *The Profession of Faith,* situates Catholic faith in the wider context of God's revelation. Then follows a treatment of the Father, Son, Spirit and Church. In answering the question 'In whom do Christians believe?', a response is offered to the human quest for meaning.

Part 2, *The Celebration of the Christian Mystery,* deals with matters liturgical and sacramental. In the thirty years since Vatican II, much good work has been done in these areas and this is well captured here. In describing how Catholics celebrate the death and resurrection of their Lord, Jesus Christ, this part gives a reply to the human quest for community.

Part 3, *Life in Christ,* deals firstly with some fundamental issues of Christian living, such as human dignity, freedom and responsibility, conscience, community, salvation and grace. And it is only in that broad context that it talks about 'loving God and loving the neighbour', since it is only in that context that the commandments and sin make sense. This whole section is a response to the human quest for life and freedom.

Part 4, *Christian Prayer,* deals with prayer in general and then offers a special treatment of the Lord's Prayer. It is a clear response to the human search for God.

Four Movements in the Symphony of the Faith (*FD* 1)

The pastoral spirit of the CCC is beautifully captured in the little logo on the cover of the book. This is an image of the god Pan, seated beneath a tree with his staff in his hand and his sheep at his feet. It seems that the early Christians liked this image so much that they used it to represent the Good Shepherd. This is a beardless Good Shepherd, with a staff for guiding and protecting his sheep; with his flute to attract his sheep by the sweet melodies of his music; and seated under a tree of life which gives shade wherever it is needed. To take that logo seriously is to know how to make good, pastoral use of the CCC. The CCC is utilised well whenever people use it to guide and protect one another, whenever they use it to attract people to Christ (426-9), whenever they use it to give shade and support to one another. The challenge before all catechists is to be true to the spirit of that logo. In this way the symphonic score of the faith will be coaxed into living music and echoes of God will be heard everywhere.

Some people may be tempted to use the CCC as a stick with which to beat others. They may take the logo on the cover rather literally: the staff becomes a stick with which to beat people. This is failing to show true pastoral sensitivity. But there is another way of using the CCC: as a shield. If we are accused of not being faithful to 'the great Tradition' (83), and if we know what is in the CCC, we can say 'but I am', or 'we are'.

The four movements in the symphony of the faith can be described as follows, by developing the theme of 'communio': We pray to a God who is a *communion* of persons; who *communicates* the inner divine life in many ways, through creation, redemption and sanctification; a Father God whose Son's Spirit is *communicated* to believers to make them one *community;* so that, in daily living, they can reflect the divine *communion* and build human *community*.

The four parts of the CCC are meant to interrelate. They are presented as an organic whole (11,18). They make no sense without one another. What is said about prayer makes no sense apart from the life of faith that supports it. What is said about the Christian mystery celebrated in liturgy makes no sense apart from the prayer life that leads up to it and the faith that inspires all of it. The life of faith, as a life of moral values, makes no sense apart from the sacramental life and the prayer life of a Christian. There is a danger of over-selectivity in reading the CCC. We might limit ourselves to reading only those parts of immediate interest to ourselves, and so we might easily fail to notice the overall pattern. In short, if we want to make sense of the CCC, we need to immerse ourselves in it, take it seriously and spend time with it. And that is not easy, because it is not an easy text to read.

However, the authors offer many aids for doing that difficult job. They give excellent cross-references (19), which help the reader to follow a theme throughout the whole book. There is also a very good analytical index at the back. Here we can find out what is dealt with and what is not, so there is no need to waste time looking for topics that are not there. Since the Word of God can provide 'a valuable working-tool in catechesis' (19), many scriptural texts are actually cited or referred to. Again, this can help in locating the sources of the teaching. Small print indicates material of lesser importance or introduces quotations from writers of importance. There are summaries at the end of each section, which are very helpful for anyone who is trying to bring things together in a synoptic way (see 278, 561, 747, 1743, 1895, 1948, 2395, 2452). For anyone who belongs to a culture where memory work is prized, this can be very helpful indeed.

The minutes of the minutes of the many meetings

As a compendium, the CCC is like blended whiskey, like those scotch whiskeys that are bland because they are blended. It lacks the fire of a single malt, it lacks the passion of an individual author. And that is the price that must be paid for a universal catechism. We rarely get the sense of an individual writer whom we can learn to love or hate. Instead, we find a bland style of writing, a soft rather than a passionate book. The CCC is an amalgamation of the insights of many different parts of our tradition: insights from the Bible and the magisterium, the patristic authors and the saints; insights from creeds and councils, synods, papal documents, encyclicals, canon law, liturgical texts, theologians, spiritual writers (a few English but no Irish). It is like a biblical concordance; all the Matthew, Mark, Luke and John together. One misses the spirit of Mark, the beauty of John. It is like the minutes of the minutes of many meetings. It is an accurate record of what went on in the Church for the last two thousand years. An accurate record that we can be sure of, but as dry as the minutes of any meeting. It lacks all the life of the meetings and it will come alive only in the hands of people who can coax it into life.

One of the best ways to do this and be faithful to the spirit of the CCC is to examine some of the pictures, in particular the four that highlight the four parts of the book.[4] These pictures are arguably more important than the actual text, because each one of them gives a certain tone or atmosphere to the section that follows, and they are all beautiful works of art. The first one (before the Creed, opposite p. 13 in both editions) is a very old fresco which shows the prophet Balaam in front of Mary and her child. Jesus, son of Mary, is the long-awaited Messiah, the hope of all

Israel. He is the centre of the Christian faith. The second picture (which comes before the Sacraments, opposite p. 237; opposite p. 222 in the pocket edition) shows a beardless Jesus and the woman with the haemorrhage clutching his cloak. This is a dynamic image of sacramental life: the life power flowing out from the Lord to heal the sickness of the world. The third picture (which comes before the Commandments, opposite p. 365; opposite p. 379 in the pocket edition) is again a beardless Jesus. This beardless Jesus is a risen Jesus, who is seated and giving the new law to Peter and Paul. Again, that is the context for the commandments and for the moral life: the new law of Christ, the risen Lord. Finally, the fourth picture (opposite p. 525; opposite p. 504 in the pocket edition) is of a bearded Christ praying to the Father, while Peter and the other disciples are looking on and trying to learn from him.

The preface to the *Roman Catechism* said that 'the whole concern of doctrine and its teaching must be directed to the love that never ends' (25). That love ought to shape the work of communicating the faith. Unless the CCC is a work of love, it will be no more than a clanging gong. It may be very beautiful, it may be a lovely work of art, but it will be a waste of time.

The CCC as a work of art

In terms of its fundamental structure, the CCC is an organic traditional presentation of the faith in terms that are relevant to believers today. The CCC can be likened to a medieval gothic cathedral. It is a beautiful work of art. And, like all medieval gothic cathedrals, one can walk around it and bring people in and show them its treasures. And there are phone-like gadgets at the doorway where people can learn more about its art. And people can get guided tours and watch the experts as they show slides and describe the various parts of the building. It is a marvellous experience, but it can lack real vitality without the people and the ceremonies for which the building has been built. Something similar can happen even with a book as beautiful and as well-produced as the CCC. It can so easily become a dead work of art, uninhabited, unvisited by people. In the Holy Land pilgrims generally visit the ruins of old churches, but then often forget the 'living stones', the people, the Arab Christians. Just as there is another way of visiting the Holy Land, there is another way of visiting the CCC. Rather than simply looking at it as a work of art and consigning it to the bookcase, we might think of visiting the people who are using it in catechesis and see how they are performing (1697).

A cellar of fine brandies

Here are a few examples of how one might draw from the CCC. A bishop could use it to find out, for example, if a new religion syllabus is adequate. Does it really measure up to the demands of the faith? Does the syllabus reflect the Trinitarian shape of the faith? (234). Is it comprehensive, or does it leave out some obvious topics?

If one wanted to preach a sermon on Mary, there is no shortage of useful material. Paragraph 487 is the classic statement of all Marian doctrine. Many references are made throughout the CCC to Mary's life, her faith, her glory as Mother of God, but above all to her role as Mother of the Church. Paragraph 971 refers to the Rosary as an 'epitome of the whole Gospel'; paragraph 1675 describes it as an extension of the liturgy; and paragraph 2678 explains how the Rosary developed in the medieval west as a popular substitute for the Prayer of the Hours.

For general Sunday homilies, any priest could get much valuable assistance, especially from the section on the mysteries of the life of Jesus (512-570), and such paragraphs as 1439 (interpretation of the parable of the Prodigal Son), 1481 (containing a Byzantine formula of absolution), and 1688 (on funeral homilies). Additional points for reflection could be found in the numerous quotations from saints and spiritual writers. Francis of Assisi's Canticle of the Creatures is cited (344). Julian of Norwich's famous dictum is quoted (313). Given the need to 'Irish' the CCC, it would be very appropriate if catechetical publishers were to provide for Irish homilists a varied selection of quotes from Irish saints as well.

If anyone wanted to offer to an ecumenical gathering a concise overview of Catholic teaching on the Eucharist, there is a very helpful section entitled 'The Sacrament of the Eucharist' (1322-1419).

Anyone teaching a lesson on Islam to a junior cycle religion class would get very little help from the CCC. However, there are a few interesting remarks about the relationship between Christianity and non-Christian religions (841-856).

A Muslim who wanted to know something about Christ would learn something from this book. The best place to begin is not the section dealing with Christ. It would be better to begin where Muslims best understand what Christians are talking about: the section on prayer (2558-2865). After seeing what is said there about the way Christians pray, the reader would automatically be brought back to an earlier part that treats of the Lord Jesus, through whom and in whom Christians pray to the Father (422-682). That would be a very good way for Muslims to find out something about Christian life.

The CCC is an excellent resource for the primary school teacher trying to prepare something on prayer. There is a fine explanation of the Psalms, of Jesus' teaching on prayer, of different forms of prayer and, especially, of the 'Our Father'. Prayer is spoken of as 'the encounter of God's thirst with ours' (2560) and we are told about words in contemplative prayer which 'are not speeches; they are like kindling that feeds the fire of love' (2717).

Senior-cycle pupils studying honesty in public life might find some very interesting material in paragraphs 2401-2463. There is material also for exploring the Christian teaching on respect for the integrity of creation (2415- 2418); the equality of women and men, created in the image of God (369-370); the problems associated with trial marriages (2391).

Any teacher of the faith – a parent, bishop, priest, or religion teacher – could draw much inspiration from paragraphs 694-701, which explain the symbols of the Holy Spirit; from paragraphs 737-741, which explain the role of the Holy Spirit in the Church, in the sacraments, in the moral life and in prayer. Paragraph 1697 should be read and reread by anybody wishing to teach Christian morality. Paragraph 2062 reminds everyone that the key to moral teaching is to show how morality is the human response to God's love. And paragraph 2082 is crucial because it reminds us that 'what God commands he makes possible by his grace'. In the context of the search for peace in Ireland, it is refreshing to read that peace is 'the stability and security of a just order' (1909).

A clear explanation of the two diverse traditions of Confirmation, in the east and in the west, is provided in paragraphs 1290-1292. There is a fascinating explanation of the first meaning of 'catholic' when applied to the Church of Jesus Christ; it means that 'in her subsists the fullness of Christ's body united with its head' (830).

What the CCC has left undone

Some people think that the new catechism will solve all our catechetical problems. That is very unlikely. It will bring us more headaches and will present us with more challenges, but it certainly will not be a panacea for all our catechetical ills. Here are some of the issues that still remain to be tackled.

1. *The need for local adaptation*

In the introduction to the *Roman Catechism* there is an extensive methodological section that explains how that book should be used.[5] The CCC has nothing as elaborate as this. All that paragraph 24 asks for is adaptation and flexibility of approach. The CCC defines itself as a definitive statement of what the Church teaches; but it is meant to be presented to people in a manner that takes account of their varied needs and their changing life situations. The Apostolic Constitution *Fidei depositum* explains the purpose of the CCC by saying that it is a compendium of Catholic doctrine, a reference book (*FD* 3). It is meant to be a point of reference for local catechisms. It is not meant to replace them; rather, they are meant to take stock of what it contains. But this is easier said than done. How is this catechism for the whole Catholic Church supposed to relate to the many local catechisms?

A similar question had already surfaced in this century. At Vatican II an effort was made to resurrect the idea of a universal catechism, which had been proposed by Vatican I, but which never got off the ground. This attempt was resisted by the Fathers of Vatican II and they opted instead for a different type of document – a directory. While a catechism tries to articulate in a comprehensive way the teachings of the faith, a directory tries to identify the principles and structures of catechesis and the guidelines for the correct use of catechisms and other resources. A directory is needed to explain how a catechism should be adapted. In calling for a directory and not a catechism, Vatican II went in a new direction (10).

The *General Catechetical Directory* (GCD)[6] was published in 1971. Its heart is section 3. The first chapter of section 3 is entitled 'Norms for the presentation of the Christian message'. Paragraphs 37-46 are critical, because they are the strictly catechetical norms which should be taken into account in any catechesis: for example, the centrality of Christ, the Trinitarian structure of the faith, the salvation dimension of the faith, the historical dimension of the faith, the obligation always to adapt catechesis to the needs of people. Anyone trying to find out how best to use the CCC won't find much help within the book itself, whereas that specific help is already available in the GCD. Paragraph 119, which deals directly with catechisms, refers back to the norms in paragraphs 37-46. The CCC is a fine text, but anybody who wants to know how to use it well will need to take account of the relevant paragraphs of the GCD, which serve as an interpretative tool for the CCC.

2. *The need for ongoing translation*

The CCC was first written in French. A very competent translation into modern idiomatic English was made by Douglas Clark, an American priest. Subsequently, this translation was abandoned in favour of a more literal translation, made by Bishop Eric Darcy. Even Darcy admits that the earlier translation was better. Though many people have lamented the unwillingness to accept the more inclusive language of the earlier translation, there is no reason to give up. Adaptation is mandated. The first kind of adaptation in many countries must surely be translation into a more inclusive idiom.

3. The need for fresh theological enterprise

It is not enough, however, to translate the words of the CCC into vernacular language in order that the deepest insights of the Catechism can be revealed. There is also a clear need for 'theological research' (94) to support the ongoing explanation of the complex and difficult themes that occur throughout the CCC. It is hoped that this book can begin the process.

4. The need for a National Catechetical Directory for Ireland

The CCC is authoritative but it is not final.[7] It took six years to prepare and is a fine piece of work. It is like a medieval gothic cathedral; but it is not the heavenly Jerusalem. A lot of construction work still remains to be done. Here in Ireland, now that the CCC has come, what we also badly need is a National Catechetical Directory for Ireland. The American Church spent five years producing its National Directory in the 1970s. It consulted far and wide and published an agreed statement of priorities.[8] An Irish Catechetical Directory could well be a similar joint enterprise of all those who are working to hand on the faith in Ireland. It would have to take account of all the insights that we have gained during the past in our work of catechesis. It would have to take seriously the centrality of adult catechesis. It would have to develop programmes for the total catechetical enterprise in Ireland, from womb to tomb. It would, therefore, have something to say to school syllabuses and textbooks. It would have recommendations for parish catechesis, for continuing faith education at third level, for ongoing ecumenical education in Ireland. It would need to offer clear guidelines for any Irish people trying to write valid and challenging catechetical material today. We don't have a catechetical directory that is specially geared to Ireland. The CCC is not one and we need one. That's where we need to go next.

FOR DISCUSSION AND REFLECTION
1. In adapting the CCC for Irish people, what changes in Irish religious culture would need to be taken into account?
2. Which topics in the CCC are better developed than they were in earlier Irish catechisms?

3. For whom should new Irish catechisms now be written?
4. Taking the example of the CCC, how could religious art be integrated into such new catechisms?

FURTHER READING

Robert J. Hater, *New Vision, New Directions: Implementing the Catechism of the Catholic Church* (Allen, Texas: Tabor Publishing, 1994).

Berard L. Marthaler (ed.), *Introducing the Catechism of the Catholic Church* (London: SPCK, 1994).

Jane E. Regan, *Exploring the Catechism* (Collegeville, Minnesota: The Liturgical Press, 1995).

Michael J. Walsh (ed.), *A Commentary on the Catechism of the Catholic Church* (London: Geoffrey Chapman, 1994).

2

SCRIPTURE IN THE CATECHISM

Michael Maher

A source of the CCC

The *Constitution on Divine Revelation* (n. 24) of Vatican II declared that 'The study of Sacred Scripture is, as it were, the soul of Sacred Theology', and went on to assert that all the Church's preaching and catechetics, and all Christian instruction, should be nourished by the word of God. In the years since Vatican II, in Ireland, as in the Church in general, the biblical movement has familiarised Catholics with the Bible and has restored the scriptures to their rightful place in the liturgical and devotional lives of the people and in the discourse of theologians. The CCC's statement about the Bible and its frequent use of biblical texts show that its authors intended to support this trend and to promote the biblical apostolate in the Church.

The Prologue to the CCC (11) informs us that the Catechism's 'principal sources are the Sacred Scriptures, the Fathers of the Church, the liturgy and the Church's Magisterium'. Among these 'principal sources' Scripture undoubtedly has pride of place. There are more than 4,100 scriptural references in the CCC, 870 from the Old Testament and 3,300 from the New Testament.[1] We may note in passing that the Documents of Vatican II, the next most frequently quoted source used in the CCC, are referred to about 800 times.

Theory and practice

In addressing the topic of Scripture in the CCC I shall attempt to answer two questions:
1. What does the CCC say at a theoretical level about Scripture and its interpretation?
2. How does the CCC itself use and interpret the Scriptures?

To answer the first question, we should turn to article 3 (101-141) of the CCC, which deals explicitly with Sacred Scripture. Here the CCC borrows heavily from *Dei verbum* (DV), the Vatican II *Constitution on Divine Revelation,* and it arranges the material in essentially the same way as that document. The introductory words to paragraphs 105-107 draw attention to the three key ideas of the passage in *Dei verbum:*
1. 'God is the author of Sacred Scripture.'
2. 'God inspired the human authors of the sacred books.'
3. 'The inspired books teach the truth.'

A new idea in the CCC is the explanation of the statement that Christianity is not a 'religion of the book' (108). Our religion has its origins in the Word made Flesh, and although the Bible is normative for Christians it is not a 'dead letter' that must be woodenly applied, but a living word that must be interpreted under the guidance of Christ who, through the Holy Spirit, 'opens our minds to understand the Scriptures' (*Lk 24:25*). The document on *The Interpretation of the Bible in the Church*, issued by the Pontifical Biblical Commission in 1993, also asserts that what the Bible says is always subject to a process of actualisation and must be continually 're-read in the light of new circumstances and applied to the contemporary situation of the People of God'.[2]

Interpreting the Scriptures

The basic principles which should be followed by the Catholic interpreter of the Scriptures are laid down in paragraphs 109-114, which take up the teaching of *Dei verbum* 12. Paragraph 109 states the general principle that the interpreter must 'be attentive to what the human authors truly wanted to affirm, and to what God wanted to reveal to us by their words'. Is 'what God wanted to reveal' the same as 'what the human authors intended to affirm'? Some scholars would answer 'yes', holding that the divine meaning of Scripture is the teaching of the writer which can be discovered by scholarly exegesis. Others would claim that what God wished to communicate can go beyond the author's meaning. That is to say, the literal sense of a text does not always convey its full theological message. This latter view is clearly the one that is adopted by the CCC, which describes the task of discovering the literal sense of a text (110), and then goes on to outline the demands of theological or ecclesial interpretation (111-14).

There is a brief discussion (110) of some of the scholarly methods that can help us to discover 'the sacred authors' intention'. Following *Dei verbum*, the CCC refers to the characteristic elements of the historical-critical method, a method that was much in vogue at the time of Vatican II.[3] One might also expect a reference in the CCC to some of the methods of biblical interpretation that have been developed and practised in the period since Vatican II. The authors might, for example, have mentioned the so-called 'narrative analysis' which 'offers a method of understanding and communicating the biblical message which corresponds to the form of story and personal testimony'.[4]

The CCC (111), which parallels a passage in *Dei verbum* 12, enunciates the principle that 'since Sacred Scripture is inspired' it 'must be … interpreted in the light of the same Spirit who inspired it'. This principle goes back to the time of the great Church Father and biblical scholar Origen (d. 254), and it is based on the conviction that since Scripture was written under the inspiration of the Holy Spirit there is a richness in the biblical text which the literal meaning does not exhaust. Guided by that same Spirit the reader may find in the text something that was not intended by the human author. Indeed, as the CCC asserts, unless the reader is guided by the Spirit, Scripture would remain 'a dead letter' and lose its relevance for the contemporary Christian.

The assertion (112) that the interpreter of the Bible must 'be especially attentive to ... the unity of the whole Scripture'[5] makes it clear that the analysis of individual passages is not enough and that any given text must be understood in the light of other biblical passages. This does not mean that one must ignore the history and formation of individual texts. It simply means that since God's plan of salvation is revealed in the whole Canon of Scripture, the interpreter must allow the final form of the Bible to shed light on its individual parts. The idea that the Bible is a unity and that the final text is the basis for theological interpretation is found throughout the whole of tradition, and in recent times it has been seen as being of fundamental importance for the proponents of some new methods of studying the Scriptures. These stress that 'the Bible is not a compilation of texts unrelated to each other; rather, it is a gathering together of a whole array of witnesses from one great Tradition. To be fully adequate to the object of its study, biblical exegesis must keep this truth firmly in mind.'[6]

The living tradition of the whole Church, which ensures the faithful transmission of the Word of God (81), must inform the interpreter of Scripture (113).[7] Very similar to this is the statement that the interpreter must be 'attentive to the analogy of faith' (114). In other words, individual affirmations of revelation or of faith must be understood in the light of the totality of the Church's teaching.[8]

In the light of Christ

To the principles enumerated in 109-114, one must add the statement which declares (129) that Christians should 'read the Old Testament in the light of Christ crucified and risen'.[9] This statement raises questions for many modern biblical scholars. They recall how the Fathers of the Church and the ecclesiastical writers had recourse to far-fetched allegorising in order to discover references to Christ in Old Testament texts,[10] and they claim that the search for Christological meanings may deprive the Hebrew scriptures of their own intrinsic value.

No one today would approve of the *excesses* of the ancient allegorists, and no one would deny that the books that have come down to us from the Old Covenant are vehicles of divine revelation independently of the Christian dispensation.[11] Nevertheless, when the earliest Christians recognised Jesus as the Messiah they could see him as the one in whom the Old Testament hopes were fulfilled. Of course, this involved a re-interpretation of the Old Testament texts. Thus, for example, Matthew (*1:23*) re-interpreted the Immanuel prophecy of Isaiah (*7:14*). In his account of Pentecost (*Acts 2:14-21*) Luke gave a new meaning to the prophecy of Joel (*2:28-32*). John re-interpreted the words 'not a bone of his shall be broken' (*Ex 12:46*) when he applied them to the death of Jesus on the Cross (*Jn 19:36*). The statement that the Flood and Noah's Ark prefigured Christian Baptism (*1 Pet 3:20-21*) involves a re-reading of Old Testament texts. Such 're-interpreting' or 're-reading' of the biblical passages discovers their 'spiritual sense', that is, 'the meaning expressed by the biblical texts when read, under the influence of the Holy Spirit, in the context of the Paschal mystery of Christ and of the new life which flows from it'.[12]

If we, following the lead of the New Testament authors, regard such a 're-reading' of the Scriptures as legitimate, 'it does not follow from this that we can attribute to a biblical verse whatever meaning we like, interpreting it in a wholly subjective way'.[13] We can discover the 'spiritual sense' only when we place a text in relation to real facts that are not foreign to it.[14] Or, to use the words of the CCC, we can 'read the Old Testament in the light of Christ' (129) provided that we remain 'attentive to what the human authors truly wanted to affirm' (109).

Scripture in the Church

Having mentioned the importance of the Scriptures for the Christian people (131) and their place in the study of theology and in the pastoral ministry of the Church (132), the text goes on to exhort all the faithful to read the Scriptures frequently in order to enrich their spiritual lives (133). Even in the years before Vatican II, biblical scholarship and the biblical apostolate were important features of the Church's life. There was a growing tendency both in theology and in spirituality to return to the Bible. Since the Council, Catholic exegetes have made important contributions to biblical scholarship, and a flood of books on biblical topics, biblical dictionaries and a great variety of periodicals has been made available to educated Catholics. Preaching and catechetical instruction have taken on a decidedly biblical tone, and Catholic spirituality has become much more scriptural than it had been in earlier times. In a sense then, paragraphs 131-133 are simply approving of what is already taking place and encouraging all Catholics to place the Bible at the centre of their spiritual lives.

Scripture in the Catechism
In the Dossier of Information issued by the editorial Commission of the CCC in 1992 it is explicitly stated that

> the Catechism does not claim to be a a work of scientific exegesis, nor does it wish to present exegetical hypotheses. Fully aware of how difficult it is, particularly today, to use Sacred Scripture correctly, the editors tried to remain faithful to the methodology indicated by *Dei verbum*, and in particular to the *analogy of Scripture,* so that a particular scripture text may be read and interpreted, with the help of the Holy Spirit, within the organic unity of the totality of Sacred Scripture, which has God for its principal author....[15]

In taking this approach the authors of the CCC are simply following the principles which they themselves have laid down (109-130). The writers of the CCC approach the Scriptures from the standpoint of the Christian faith and their interests are primarily theological, ecclesial and devotional. But they are not indifferent to the insights of professional biblical scholars, and the *Dossier* just quoted goes on to say that the biblical quotations in the CCC were carefully examined by a team of exegetes. We do not know who these exegetes were, but we do know that many exegetes who have commented on the CCC have failed to give their wholehearted approval to the way in which biblical quotations and references are used by its authors. One German scholar had the following to say:

> To put it bluntly, for a biblical scholar, or for anyone who is familiar with the problems relating to the Bible, reading the Catechism is a Way of the Cross. Since the Church in her most authoritative pronouncements has not only allowed, but positively encouraged the use of the historical-critical method in the interpretation of the Bible, one would expect to find signs in a Church document of such status as the Catechism that this method has been applied by its authors. But one finds few indications that such is the case.[16]

Examining some texts
The author just quoted does not give specific examples to illustrate his point. So let us now, within the limited space available, examine a few texts that might help us to evaluate his negative stance. We can begin with some numbers from the section on prayer, the section which is generally regarded as the best in the CCC.

The first biblical reference in this section is to Psalm 130:1 which is mentioned in footnote 3 (2559). The opening words, 'Out of the depths', which are quoted in the CCC, may originally have referred to the sufferings and misfortunes that overwhelmed the psalmist. However, since the psalmist goes on to refer to sin and forgiveness (vv. 3-4) and to his own patient confidence in the Lord (vv. 5-6), the words 'Out of the depths I cry to you' can, as happens in the CCC, be understood as an urgent prayer arising from a humble and contrite heart. St Augustine saw Psalm 130 as the prayer of a sinner who acknowledged his poverty in the presence of God, and St Gregory the Great regarded it as an expression of humility.

The next two quotations, from Luke 18:9-14 and Romans 8:26, are entirely appropriate in the context, and they are used in the CCC according to their obvious meaning (2559).

Things are not so straightforward when we turn our attention to the next paragraphs (2560-2561). Does paragraph 2560 offer a genuine application of the phrase 'If you had known the gift of God' (*Jn 4:10*), with which the paragraph opens? At a *homiletic* level the CCC's application of the story of the Samaritan woman is perfectly understandable. The woman who came seeking water can be seen as representing all of us who come seeking Jesus. Jesus is the one who is always thirsting to meet us in prayer. He takes the initiative and enters into dialogue with us. He is always ready to offer us 'the gift of God' and to enrich us with 'living water'. It is he who answers our prayer when, like the Samaritan woman, we say 'Give me to drink'.

But does this homiletic application reflect the *intention* of the author of John 4? Or is it a matter of reading our concepts of prayer back into John's story? I have read several commentaries on this chapter and none of them refers to prayer. When explaining the term 'the gift of God' (quoted in paragraph 2560) and the phrase 'living water' (in paragraph 2561), Raymond Brown states that it has been popular among systematic theologians since medieval times to treat 'living water' as a symbol for sanctifying grace. Brown himself maintains that, within the scope of Johannine theology, there are really only two possibilities:
1. 'Living water' refers to Jesus' revelation or teaching;
2. 'Living water' is the Spirit communicated by Jesus.

Brown says that both meanings were probably intended. There may also be, he says, a secondary reference to Baptism in the text.[17] The German scholar Schnackenburg, whose massive three-volume commentary on John has been translated into English, says that the 'living water' which Jesus has to offer is 'his revelation and the divine life which he communicates'.[18]

None of these commentators refers to prayer, and we must take it that John 4:10, to which the authors of paragraphs 2560-61 of the CCC appeal, does not refer to prayer. Perhaps then the CCC is, according to its own principles, interpreting the Gospel verse in the light of 'the Tradition of the Church'. As St Augustine is quoted (2560), I decided to check the text mentioned in footnote 8 to see if there is a reference there to prayer. The phrase in the CCC, 'God thirsts that we may thirst for him' is true to the spirit of Augustine's words. But Augustine says nothing about prayer. He says that the Lord thirsted for the woman's faith, so that when she was thirsty he would give her the Holy Spirit. Augustine then quotes John 7:37-39 ('… "out of the believer's heart shall flow rivers of living water". Now he said this about the Spirit which believers in him were to receive') and makes the point that the living waters signify the gift of the Spirit which the Lord was to give to the Church after his glorification.

It seems then that neither the literal sense of John 4:10 nor Augustine's explanation of that verse gives a solid basis for the CCC's linking of that particular text with prayer. The authors did not derive their teaching from St John's text. They read their own teaching back into the evangelist's words. One can allow this in popular preaching and teaching, but in an authoritative Church document like the CCC, which should teach people how to handle the biblical text correctly, we have the right to expect a more nuanced interpretation of the Gospel story.

Linkword composition

Moving on to footnote 10 of paragraph 2561 we may ask how Jeremiah 2:13 supports the CCC's teaching on prayer. In fact, Jeremiah's words have nothing whatsoever to do with prayer. They form part of a very moving passage (2:9-13) in which the prophet condemns the folly of his people who have abandoned God, who is a 'fountain of living water', and put their trust in gods who are as useless as leaking cisterns. Jeremiah's words are out of place in the CCC, and they have been dragged into it only by a kind of 'linkword' or 'catchword' composition. The mention of 'living water' in John 4:10 prompted the editors to refer to Jeremiah, who also refers to 'living water', which he contrasts with cisterns that hold no water. This kind of association of texts which had totally different meanings in their original contexts is unjustifiable.

The heart of prayer

The CCC claims that Scripture refers more than a thousand times to the heart as the source of prayer, and then goes on to say that 'according to

Scripture it is the *heart* that prays' (2562). This seems to ignore the fact that in the Bible all the emotions of which a person is capable may be attributed to the heart. The heart is glad (*Prov 27:11*); rejoices (*Ps 13:5*); is sad (*Neh 2:2*); sorry (*Ps 13:2*); courageous (*2 Sam 17:10*); defiant (*Deut 2:30*); hardened (*Ps 95:8*) etc. In the light of all this it may not be very meaningful to say that the heart is the source of prayer. Furthermore, texts that might seem to refer to prayer in the heart may not in fact do so. See, for example, 1 Sam 1:12-13 (RSV): 'As she continued praying ... Hannah was speaking in her heart'. But this simply means that '... Hannah was praying silently', and this is in fact the translation in the NRSV. See also 2 Chronicles 12:24; Job 11:13. There are, of course, texts that explicitly associate the heart with various kinds of prayers; cf. Psalms 9:1; 19:14; 84:2; Mark 7:6; Luke 2:19. 51. But I doubt very much if 'more than a thousand' such texts could be listed.

To say that 'prayer is a covenant relationship between God and man' (2564) is to take the term 'covenant' in a very broad and unusual sense. The CCC treats of the covenants with Noah (56, 58, 1080), Abraham (72), Moses (62, 2810), and of the Old Covenant (28, 2811) and the New Covenant (64, 73, 762). In these texts the term 'covenant' has a rich theological meaning. It seems to me that to speak of prayer as a covenant is to take liberties with that term and to debase its meaning.

Unfinished business

In the *Dossier of Information,* quoted above, the authors of the CCC state clearly that they did not set out to produce a work of scientific exegesis. Even without such a statement no one would expect a catechism to reflect all the ins and outs of modern biblical scholarship. It would therefore be wrong to apply the standards of rigorous scientific exegesis to the CCC's every use of scriptural texts. Nevertheless, our respect for a Roman document of such importance as the CCC should not prevent us from reading it with a critical eye and evaluating it from different angles.

In the first part of this chapter, I discussed what the CCC says at a theoretical level about Scripture and its interpretation in the Church. My reflections could be summed up by saying that in paragraphs 101-141 the CCC outlines the characteristics of Catholic biblical interpretation. This interpretation must always be guided by scientific research and must take place within the living tradition of the Church and under the guidance of the Spirit. In developing those points, the CCC remains faithful to the teaching of *Dei verbum,* but it adds almost nothing to the teaching of that document. On reading this section of the CCC one might well ask if biblical scholarship has stood still for the thirty years that have passed since the promulgation of *Dei verbum.* When the statements of the Pontifical Biblical Commission's document on *The Interpretation of the Bible in the Church,* to which I have referred several times, are compared with those of the CCC, the limits of the latter become apparent. The Biblical Commission's presentation shows an openness to new methods of biblical interpretation and to the problems of presenting the Scriptures in the contemporary world, an openness that is lacking in the CCC.

Limitations of space have allowed me to deal only with a few biblical texts that are used in one short introductory section of the CCC. But I hope that what I have written will help to promote an awareness of some of the strengths and weaknesses of the CCC's use of the Scripture. An obvious *strength* of the CCC is, as some of the references which we have discussed show, that it frequently uses apt scriptural passages to support and justify its theological statements. Its generous use of biblical quotations and references will also have the effect of familiarising people with the word of God. But a stringing together of texts that may have different meanings in their biblical contexts must be considered a *weak* point, since such a procedure displays an indifference to the authentic significance of each text. Even when the CCC uses only one or just a few texts to bolster its arguments, it can sometimes depart from the original meaning of the text, and it is this kind of procedure that has given rise to the disquiet of some Scripture scholars. My comments in the second part show that I share this disquiet to some extent. However, scholars have not yet begun a systematic examination of the CCC's use of Scripture, and I am sure that in the near future many books and articles will treat us to discussions on this topic.

FOR DISCUSSION AND REFLECTION
1. Does the CCC give a sufficiently prominent place to the Scriptures?
2. Does its application of scriptural texts always reflect their true meaning?
3. Outline what you see as some of the strengths and weaknesses of the CCC's use of the Scriptures.
4. Is the CCC's teaching on original sin faithful to the true meaning of the Scriptures?
5. Does the CCC help to foster a biblical spirituality?

FURTHER READING
The Interpretation of the Bible in the Church, Address of His Holiness Pope John Paul II and the Document of the Pontifical Biblical Commission (Rome: Vatican Press, 1993).

J. Jensen, 'Beyond the Literal Sense. The interpretation of the Scriptures in the Catholic Church', *The Living Light* 29 (summer 1993), pp. 50-60.

J. E. Regan, *Exploring the Catechism* (Collegeville, Minnesota: The Liturgical Press, 1995), pp. 71-78.

3.

I BELIEVE – WE BELIEVE
Faith and Doctrine in the Catechism

Eoin G. Cassidy

God's invitation

There is a story told of a priest who, in the days of the old *Maynooth Catechism*, caused consternation in his parish by his unorthodox way of examining the children on the Catechism. Instead of reading out a question and asking for an answer he used to read out an answer and ask the children for the appropriate question. In his opinion, it was easy to learn off the answers, harder to learn off the questions, and harder still, but much more important, to account for them. The CCC differs from the *Maynooth Catechism* in many respects, one of them being that it does not provide any questions. The task facing readers of the CCC is to supply the questions or, more precisely, to be sensitive to the living questions, the questions that are appropriate in the concreteness and particularity of the here and now. That is the difficult but indispensable task facing each one of us as we respond to the challenge of communicating our faith to pupils, parishioners, family, friends and colleagues, and, most importantly, as we endeavour to teach ourselves, every day anew, the meaning of our faith. This chapter will attempt to uncover the questions which motivated those who wrote the section in the CCC on faith, entitled 'I Believe – We Believe'. It will also endeavour to supply the questions which daily confront those who seek to understand and profess the Christian faith in the Ireland of the last decade of the twentieth century – a society increasingly marked by the culture of a secular and consumerist ethos.

The dialogue that is faith is a dialogue with God, a dialogue with the Church, a dialogue with the wider secular world and, finally, in some sense, a dialogue with one's own experiences and innermost feelings. Each of us approaches the issue of faith from our own perspective, we come with our own questions, those which have been chiselled out of our particular experience. Is it possible to show my child the credibility of belief or the value of belief? Why is it that so many people I know have lost the faith or at least seem indifferent to it? How can I continue to believe as I see my closest friend/partner suffer such a painful illness? Can I believe in

God without believing in the Church? Is it just my imagination or have the beliefs which constitute the Catholic faith changed since Vatican II?

God's invitation and our response, within which faith finds its place, has three moments – all of which find their unity in the possibility of receiving and responding to God's self-revelation to us in the incarnation. It is this truth which explains the structure of the section in the CCC on faith, a section which is divided into three chapters. The first, 'Man's capacity for God', and the third, 'Man's response to God', find their focus only in the light of the second chapter, 'God comes to meet man'.

Man's capacity for God

The concern underlying this first section is to show the reasonableness of faith. It is a very understandable concern, because the possibility of dialogue with those seeking to understand the Christian faith is dependent on our ability to show that there is an openness in the human being to receive God's revelation. The issue for each of us in our pluralist and increasingly secular environment in Ireland is to account for our faith to ourselves as well as to those to whom we minister. We have to show that the truth of God's revelation can be recognised by us either because it meets our deepest needs, confirms our highest aspirations, or concurs with the way in which we experience the world. If there was no link between reason and revelation or between nature and grace we would have no possibility of recognising God and, furthermore, no reason to receive God's revelation.

In responding to this concern to offer a credible account of what motivates a person to believe in God, one whom he or she has never seen, the authors of the CCC alert us, albeit in summary form, to some of the things which define us as human beings. Under the heading of 'The Desire for God' (27-30) they remind us that as God comes to meet us he does not appear as a stranger, because the desire for God is written in our hearts. Quoting that memorable passage from the *Confessions* of St Augustine, 'You have made us for yourself, O Lord, and our hearts are restless until they rest in you'(30), they alert us to what each one of us recognises: namely, that there is a yearning in us all to know the truth about ourselves and about the world in which we live, a yearning for truth and a search for happiness and peace, one which in every generation and in every culture has found expression in the search for God.

The desire for God may be written in the hearts of all people in every generation, but the question remains: does anything correspond to this desire? Is it just wishful thinking, a continuation of every child's dream for a father/mother figure? Perhaps God is a phantasm which we invent to dull the pain of human deprivation or to mitigate the many disappointments which accompany human life as it is experienced. Under the heading 'Ways of Coming to Know God' (31-35) the authors attempt to address this issue. Drawing upon the rich philosophical heritage which is the legacy of Christianity they point to 'converging and convincing' arguments which allow us to attain certainty about the truth of God's existence. These arguments can be classified under two headings corresponding to two different starting-points, i.e. the objective world and the human subject. The former reflects upon the fact that we encounter the world as an intelligible, ordered and purposeful world. Furthermore, it recognises the contingency of existence, the realisation that the world does not contain within itself the reason for its own existence. Finally, it acknowledges our ability to experience the world as beautiful. All of these point us inexorably towards the acceptance of God as the origin and goal of the world as it is experienced. In the course of their treatment of this theme the authors of the CCC quote a fine passage from one of the sermons of St Augustine which reminds us that, despite the transient character of this earthly existence, we receive in the experience of beauty a glimpse of a world that is not subject to decay; in the experience of beauty we receive a trace or a footprint of the one who is Beauty itself, namely God. Just as art draws us to praise the artist, so, likewise, the recognition of beauty draws us to praise the creator of beauty (32).

In the same section the CCC offers us a glimpse of yet another path which can lead to the acknowledgement of the existence of God. It draws attention to the fact that at some level of our experience each of us is touched not only by the desire for truth and beauty and a sense of moral goodness, but also by the freedom and voice of conscience and a longing for happiness. In these experiences we can discern signs of the seed of eternity which we bear in ourselves, signs which can have their origin only in God.

God comes to meet man

If the first chapter treated of the capacity of the human person to receive God's revelation, the second chapter, 'God comes to meet Man', focuses on the topic of revelation itself. Questions which we may bring to this chapter include the following: What is the content of revelation or the deposit of the faith? How do we know what we are asked to believe? To what extent is one obliged to believe in such things as the Church, the communion of saints, heaven and hell? Perhaps the question will be put in the form of a statement like the following: 'My faith is in Christ and/or in the Bible but I do not believe in doctrine nor do I believe in the Church.' The authors of the CCC were sensitive to these concerns. This can be seen through an analysis of the content of the chapter which is structured both to highlight the Christocentric focus of revelation and to ensure that readers both understand the relation between scripture and tradition, and acknowledge the role of the Magisterium in preserving the deposit of the faith.

In the course of their treatment of the Christocentric focus of all revelation (51-53 and 65-67) the authors of this section of the CCC quote this beautiful passage from the writings of St John of the Cross:

> In giving us his Son, his only Word (for he possesses no other), he spoke everything to us at once in this sole Word – and he has no more to say... because what he spoke before to the prophets in parts, he has now spoken all at once by giving us the All Who is His Son. Any person questioning God or desiring some vision or revelation would be guilty not only of foolish behaviour but also of offending him, by not fixing his eyes entirely upon Christ and by living with the desire for some other novelty (65).

Apart from providing an authoritative perspective from which to question those engaged in the needless and vain search for some special source of additional revelation, the passage provides the basis for the acceptance of a hierarchy of truths. As the CCC states:

> The mutual connections between dogmas, and their coherence, can be found in the whole of the Revelation of the mystery of Christ. 'In Catholic doctrine there exists an order or "hierarchy" of truths, since they vary in their relation to the foundation of the Christian faith'. (90)

Our faith is in Christ and Christ alone. This is not to state that such beliefs as the Church, the communion of saints, heaven and hell do not form part of the deposit of the faith. On the contrary, the deposit of the faith includes a whole range of truths which are integral to the Christian faith. What the authors of the CCC wished to reaffirm is the traditional teaching of the Catholic Church, namely, that all truths must be seen in the light of God's self-revelation in Christ. For instance, we believe in the Church understood as the Body of Christ; likewise Mary, seen as the mother of God. The acceptance of the dogmas of the Church is essential to the lived expression of the Christian faith precisely because dogmas expose truths which have a necessary connection with the self-revelation of God in Christ.

A key premise of Catholic teaching and one of its distinguishing characteristics is the conviction that the revelation of Christ is communicated as a living Gospel to each generation through the tradition of the Church as well as through the Sacred Scriptures. There is one common source, the Holy Spirit, but two distinct paths of transmission. Quoting extensively from the Vatican II document *Dei verbum,* the CCC reaffirms this Catholic viewpoint that 'the Church, to whom the transmission and interpretation of revelation is entrusted, "does not derive her certainty about all revealed truths from the holy Scriptures alone" '(82). However, the CCC is equally concerned to emphasise the close relation between Scripture and tradition (80-82). If one accepts the Pauline image of the Church as the Body of Christ there can never be any question of a conflict between Scripture and tradition. Furthermore, it is in this context that the CCC situates the task of the Magisterium of the Church, that is the authority and responsibility of the Pope and the bishops in communion with him, to interpret faithfully both Scripture and tradition. As the CCC puts it, 'Yet this Magisterium is not superior to the Word of God, but is its servant' (86).

The CCC speaks of the Church's Magisterium exercising the authority it holds from Christ to the fullest extent when it defines dogmas. In acknowledging the importance of dogma, the CCC takes care to stress the connection between our spiritual life and the dogmas of the Church. Dogmas are seen in the context of the need for 'lights along the path of faith' (89). This is not only a fine image but one that allows us to grasp the role of dogma. What must be stressed, particularly as we read a Catechism which is laid out in a series of propositions, is that our faith is not in these propositions or dogmas. Our faith is in the person of Christ, who is revealed through the aid of dogma. As long as we are sensitive to this Christocentric focus of all dogmas we will be able to situate them in their proper context, as priceless aids to both the understanding and communication of the faith as it lives and grows in the life of the Church.

Man's response to God

It is in the third and final chapter in this section, 'Man's response to God', that we are introduced to a detailed treatment of faith understood as the appropriate response to God's revelation. There is a whole range of questions which could be brought to a study of this chapter, questions such as: What does it mean to respond to God in faith? Can faith in a loving God be reconciled with the existence of the suffering of innocent people? Can faith in God be reconciled with the discoveries of science? Is faith necessary for salvation? Is faith compatible with doubt? To whom may we turn as a model of the faith?

What are the questions and concerns which the authors of the CCC brought to this chapter on faith? Undoubtedly, the principal concern which influenced the structuring of this chapter was the desire to ensure that readers would understand faith in the context of the drama created by the dialectic between grace and free will. One of the central pillars of the Christian religion is the belief that both the revelation of God in Jesus Christ and our response to that revelation in faith have their origin in grace, that is, in the love of God. Not only is God's revelation to us received as a gift of God's love but our response to God in faith is equally an act of grace. Faith in God can never be attained purely by the use of human reason, no matter how finely attuned it may be (153).

Questions then emerge as to why we regard faith as a virtue or why it is that we praise the person of faith. If faith is a gift from God what role is there for the person in the process of responding to God in faith? In answering, the CCC is careful to stress that the gift of faith is not one that coerces. On the contrary, God's gift is one which respects the freedom of each person to accept or to reject it (160). This issue of how to explain the relation between grace and free will is a complex one, and, furthermore, one which was central to the controversy which sundered the unity of the Church at the time of the Reformation. In keeping with the tradition of the Catholic Church, the CCC emphasises the importance of free will, and thus the contribution which each person has the freedom to make while moving to the goal for which we are created.

The second concern of the authors of the CCC in writing this chapter was to stress the reasonableness of faith. While acknowledging the graced character of revelation, they emphasise that there is, in principle, no conflict between the world of faith and the world of science (156-159). This is an important point because, all too often in our contemporary culture, the world of science and the world of religion are presented as being mutually exclusive.

In laying emphasis on the reasonableness of faith there is, however, always the temptation to overlook those experiences such as the suffering of innocent human beings, which seem to contradict our faith in a loving God. The CCC is careful to avoid any suggestion that faith can be reduced to reason and, in this context, it acknowledges that experiences such as these pose a great challenge to our faith:

> If God the Father almighty, the Creator of the ordered and good world, cares for all his creatures, why does evil exist? To this question, as pressing as it is unavoidable and as painful as it is mysterious, no quick answer will suffice.... There is not a single aspect of the Christian message that is not in part an answer to the question of evil. (309)

This is a theme which recurs in other parts of the CCC and reflects a keen awareness that faith and reason will never, in this life, be fully reconciled. Not that this should surprise us, considering that the Christian faith is based upon the story of the innocent One who was crucified out of love for us. Christianity may stand dumb before the terrifying mystery of evil, but it is not based on the pretence that evil and the suffering of innocent people do not exist. The Christian's faith is not in a God who is distant from, or indifferent to, the drama of human existence, a God who is distant from the deprivations and suffering that make so many lives a living crucifixion. The God of the Christian faith is one who is closest to those who are innocent victims of human injustice, precisely because he knew what it was to suffer as an innocent victim. The God we believe in is, literally speaking, the one who is compassionate.

One of the most rewarding aspects of this chapter in the CCC is the way it introduces us to the models of faith. For those of us exercised by the question of what it is to be a person of faith in the Ireland of the late twentieth century, we could do worse than to reflect on the lives of those figures who are presented to us as models of faith, namely, the Old Testament figure of Abraham, the person of Mary the mother of God and the figure of Jesus himself (145-149, 165). Drawing attention to these three key figures in the drama of faith allows us to recognise the importance of the will in the act of faith. In all three cases, faith is presented in the context of a clear choice. Abraham could have refused to follow God's invitation to leave his land, family and father's house and, at the age of seventy-five, travel to an unknown land. Mary could have refused to accept the invitation to be the mother of God. And, finally, as Jesus' prayer to the Father in the Garden of Gethsemane illustrates, it was open to him to refuse to receive the cup of sorrow which he had been asked to accept for our sakes.

Faith is not only a matter of one's own free will but, just as importantly, it is an act of obedience to the will of God. As the CCC points out, we are conscious that in all cases Abraham's silent and unshakeable faith was rooted in an unquestioning obedience to God's will. Even the supreme test of faith which God placed before him, namely, the command to sacrifice his son Isaac, was accepted without a single word of dissent. It is the silence of Abraham which testifies to his unquestioning obedience. Equally, it is the silence of Mary before the cross which allows us a privileged insight into this quality of her faith, understood as obedience to the will of God. This acceptance of God's authority which we first see in the words of Mary: 'I am the handmaid of the Lord, let what you have said be done to me' (*Lk 1:38*), finds its echo in that great prayer of faith which her son Jesus spoke in the garden of Gethsemane, one which concludes with the words: 'let your will be done, not mine' (*Lk 22:43*). Faith is an exercise of the will but, more precisely, it is a submission of the will to the will of God. In the last analysis, although faith may be reasonable it is not based on reason, rather it is based on the decision to accept the authority of God (156).

As even a cursory glance at the figures of Abraham, Mary and Jesus shows, there is no half-way stage between the acceptance and rejection of faith. However, as each of us can testify, faith cannot avoid what St John of the Cross calls the dark night of the soul – those moments when we are struck by the seeming paradox or absurdity of faith rather than its reasonableness. Abraham before his son Isaac on the altar of wood, Mary before her son Jesus on the cross of wood, must both have sensed the paradox of faith. Likewise, Jesus, as he uttered that cry 'My God, my God, why hast thou forsaken me?' (*Mt 27:46*). To the untutored ear it must have sounded like the cry of despair. In fact, it is the cry of one who refused to despair, the cry of one who refused to heed the taunts of the onlookers to come down off the cross and save himself. Faith can at times show itself as a stubborn, almost irrational refusal to abandon belief. The faith of Jesus on the cross is none other than an example of this refusal to despair, and, interestingly, in this refusal, it reminds us of how close faith is to the virtue of hope. One finds a beautiful expression of this link between faith and hope in St Paul's letter to the Romans as he speaks of Abraham in the following words: 'Hoping against hope he believed, and thus became the father of many nations'(*Rom 4:18*).

The CCC offers a fine portrayal of the models of faith and acknowledges the link between faith and hope which St Paul highlights when speaking of Abraham. In doing so, it is not unmindful of the difficulties attending the acceptance of faith, difficulties which are, at some stage, experienced by all believers, and sensed with a particular intensity in the lives of Abraham, Mary[1] and, above all, her son, Jesus (164-165).

Faith and hope are clearly linked, but what of the connection between faith and love? For many, it is this link which, above all, gives us a privileged access to the mystery of faith. For instance, we readily recognise that love is incomprehensible unless the related motifs of faithfulness and trust are acknowledged. Love is not possible if we have no faith or trust, or if we are unfaithful. Is it possible, however, to have faith without love? Undoubtedly, we can be motivated by fear but, if that fear excludes love, it is not a 'faithful' response in any meaningful sense of that term. The CCC clearly acknowledges that faith is a response of the whole person, both intellect and will, to the call of Christ. Surprisingly there is little in this section to alert us to richness of the link between faith and love and the way in which this link can help us to grasp the true nature of faith as a response to God's love.²

I believe – we believe

Is faith simply a matter of my relationship with God? To what extent are we obliged to recognise that there is a communitarian dimension to the Christian faith? The CCC faces up squarely to this issue in the last part of this chapter, 'We Believe'. In marked contrast to the individualist ethos of the developed world, the CCC grounds its conviction for the necessity of the Church in a relational anthropology, namely, a vision of human nature that recognises that we have not been created to live as isolated individuals but that we live and grow as members of a community (162).

To suppose that faith concerns simply myself and God not only manifests a striking indifference both to the concerns of others and to concern for others, but also reflects ignorance of the way in which values and beliefs are acquired. These are acquired in and through the community, namely, the family and the wider community in which we live. Similarly, it is of the utmost importance to recognise that we belong to a faith community, and that the Church is in essence a faith community. To ignore the Church is fundamentally to misunderstand the way in which God's revelation is communicated. The love of Christ is communicated through the Church as the 'body of Christ'. Furthermore, the Church is not only important as the community wherein we receive faith but also as the community through which we can express and celebrate our faith (168).

Interestingly, it is in this context that the CCC offers the finest rationale for the presence of dogma. It is only in and through the shared acceptance and proclamation of faith as expressed in creed (the Apostles' Creed or the Nicene Creed) that we can both recognise and celebrate our faith as members of a community of believers. We do not believe in propositions but it is the formulations of the faith which enable us, as the CCC says: 'to express the faith and to hand it on, to celebrate it in community, to assimilate and live on it more and more'(170). Most importantly, the dogmas and creeds of the Church give expression to the unity of the Christian faith. Quoting from the writings of the second century Father of the Church, St Irenaeus of Lyons, the CCC states:

> Indeed, the Church, though scattered throughout the whole world, even to the ends of the earth, having received the faith from the apostles and their disciples ... guards [this preaching and faith] with care,

as dwelling in but a single house, and similarly believes as if having but one soul and a single heart, and preaches, teaches and hands on this faith with a unanimous voice, as if possessing only one mouth. (173)

It is a beautiful passage which, drawing on images which can be found in Psalm 67:7 and Acts 4:32, allows us to feel the intensity of Irenaeus' love for the unity of the Church and the importance in this context of a shared creed and shared doctrine, both of which enable us to speak from every corner of the world, as if possessing only one mouth. Incidentally, the importance of witnessing to the the unity of the faith is a testimony to the abiding value of a catechism.

Conclusion: What still remains to be done

As is obvious from the above, the CCC offers an accurate portrayal of Catholic teaching in a format which is accessible to the non-specialist in theology. However, while acknowledging the value of the CCC, one must be sensitive to the limitations which the Catechism format imposes on the authors. There are three areas in which the reader could benefit from a more lengthy analysis than that provided by the CCC.

Firstly, in terms of the challenge of ecumenism which faces us today, it is important to be conscious of the importance of this section of the CCC. The topics treated, namely, nature and grace, scripture and tradition, grace and free will, are the very ones which gave rise to the controversies which caused the Reformation and still divide the Catholic Church from the Protestant denominations. It may not be the function of the CCC to offer a treatise on the roots of the Reformed tradition. Nevertheless, it will be difficult to have a sense of the significance of this section without some background reading in this area.

For example, on the issue of natural theology or, more precisely, the statement of Vatican I which is repeated in chapter one of this section of the CCC, namely, that we can come to know with certainty the existence of God by the light of human reason alone, it must be recognised that many, apart from those of the Protestant denominations, have difficulty in interpreting this dogma in a manner that respects the graced character of creation. The Catholic position gives expression to the conviction that grace builds upon nature. What must also be recognised is that it is an equally Catholic position to hold that nature supposes grace. If creation is an act of God's love it follows that there is no such thing as a state of pure nature; all human life from the moment of conception is graced. What this signifies is that the personal gift of God to us in Christ, expressed in and through the incarnation, is the ultimate foundation of the very existence of the world and human beings existing in the world.[3]

The second point relates to the relation between faith and dogma. While acknowledging that faith needs to be expressed in propositions we must constantly be aware of the danger of identifying faith with dogma, and, indeed, of the danger of identifying faith with a catechism. To know one's faith is not to know one's catechism, rather it is to know God, or, more precisely, it is to know and to love God. While the CCC clearly acknowledges this truth, we could question whether it places enough emphasis on the relational character of faith. Faith in God is synonymous with a relationship of trust which has its roots in our love of God. Furthermore, a faith which does not overflow in charity and which does not find expression in work for social justice is a contradiction.[4] This is not to deny the importance of dogmas. However, an over-emphasis on the intellectual dimension of faith risks losing sight of the multi-faceted character of human nature; faith is a response of the whole person.

The third point focuses upon the difficulties attending the acceptance of faith or, more precisely, upon the question of whether faith and doubt can co-exist. As mentioned above, the CCC acknowledges the many factors which can make it difficult to accept faith. However, there is no indication that the CCC would accept the co-existence of faith and doubt. Does this adequately reflect the way in which faith is lived in the concrete? Unlike the refusal of faith, which involves a clear decision, doubt is rarely perceived in such clear-cut terms as an act of the will. For the most part it is seen rather as an experience which can accompany decisions or predispose us to refrain from deciding. There are many whose strong faith can be accompanied by great doubt. There are many who could echo the words of the man recorded by St Luke, 'Lord, I believe, help my unbelief'. The importance of this point is, that if we see faith in terms of a relationship rather than as an intellectual assent to truth, we will recognise that faith is never something achieved once and for all. Faith, like trust, is a challenge which is always before us. The challenge of responding to Christ's love in faith is not just to accept faith but to grow in faith. St Luke's account of Our Lord's encounter with the disciples on the road to Emmaus offers us a sensitive treatment of this issue. We do not expect the CCC to give a psychological account of the stages a person goes through on the road to faith, but for the reader who is interested in understanding the drama of faith, the CCC would need to be complemented by a study of the steps to faith and the barriers preventing its acceptance.[5] In this context, it should not be forgotten that there is an inescapable link between the acceptance of faith and the need for conversion.

Clearly, no single, brief chapter on faith is capable of doing justice to the questions which we might bring to the issue of faith, and if we read this chapter in isolation from other sections in the Catechism which treat of faith we will inevitably be disappointed. One of the most enriching aspects of the CCC is the provision by the authors of an extensive list of cross-references. Taking the trouble to make use of the cross-references in this chapter on faith will more than repay the effort involved. It is only possible fully to appreciate the CCC teaching on this issue in conjunction with those references. In this way, we can seek to discern how the Church's understanding of faith both informs and is informed by the full range of Christian teaching. Provided we are sensitive to the nature and limitations of a catechism and take the trouble to read any section of the CCC in the light of the rest of it, we will find this section a precious aid to the understanding and communication of the Catholic faith.

FOR DISCUSSION AND REFLECTION
1. Is it possible to offer a credible account of what motivates a person to believe in God, one whom he or she has never seen?
2. To what extent does the CCC address the problems associated with faith which are encountered in Ireland in the late twentieth century?
3. Discuss the multi-faceted nature of the relation between faith and dogma.
4. What is the significance of this section for contemporary ecumenical dialogue?

FURTHER READING

Henri De Lubac, *The Sources of Revelation* (New York: Herder and Herder, 1968).

Avery Dulles, *The Survival of Dogma: Faith, Authority and Dogma in a Changing World* (New York: Crossroad, 1987).

Michael Paul Gallagher, *Struggles of Faith* (Dublin: The Columba Press, 1990).

John Macquarrie, *Invitation to Faith* (London: SCM Press, 1994).

4

THE PROFESSION OF
THE CHRISTIAN FAITH: THE CREEDS

Breandán Leahy

Tell me about your God
On a long train journey some years ago I found myself sitting opposite an avid reader. When we struck up a conversation it transpired that he had a passion for philosophy. Heidegger and Camus were recently discovered intrigues. At a certain point he turned to me and, while explaining his own inability to really believe in God and the Church, he said, 'Who is God for you? Tell me about your God.'

In many ways in Ireland today, we are all being invited to tell each other about our God. Interacting with the EU, regional funds, Beef Tribunals, peace initiatives, X-Cases, media scandals, education debates, the Nuclear Non-Proliferation Treaty, New Age, bio-ethical questions and moral debates, an invitation is being issued to enter a new 'communion of soul', sharing, as perhaps never before, where we are in our relationship with God.

We are beginning to realise that what we are living through is, in some ways, a delayed effect of the Enlightenment experienced on continental Europe some two centuries ago. Our religion speaks of a discovery of God. We have a revealed religion, one which is shared by millions, both in our country and around the world. And yet, somehow, in the name of science and rationality, it often occurs that the availability of a light and wisdom which comes from divine revelation is limited to the level of personal inspiration. Often people are not aware of how our Creed can provide a profound meaning for our lives at all levels.

Michael Paul Gallagher speaks of a 'new agenda' facing us in Ireland today, not merely in terms of catechesis and preaching, but, most importantly, in terms of Christian living itself.[1] G. K. Chesterton's description of Catholicism in Ireland at the time of the 1932 Eucharistic Congress makes interesting reading today:

> Her religion has always been poetic, popular and, above all, domestic. Nobody who knows anything of her population will think there was ever any special danger that her Deity would be only a definition. He was always so intimate as rather to resemble, in a pagan par-

allel, a household god or a family ghost. Ireland was filled with the specially human spirit of Christianity, especially in the sense of the pathetic, the sensitive and the great moral emotions that attach to memory.[2]

Maybe there is still no danger that God is only a definition in Ireland, but we are faced with a strange paradox. Just as the practical corollaries of who we say God is loom larger in importance than ever before because of the many new issues facing us, less seems to be known about our God and God's plans as revealed in Jesus Christ. While not yet reaching the mass cultural indifference or atheism of continental Europe, we too have entered a systematic rejection of the 'household' God and the 'family's' Church. At the same time, we sense in some a search for a God who is 'home' for us in a modern manner, and a 'family' where relationships between us all, children, women, men, religious, priests, bishops and Pope, are authentic, mature, and 'one in Christ'.

A 'new Ireland' needs a new discovery of who God really is. Both Vatican II[3] and the 1991 Synod on Europe have suggested the need to present, in a new and more authentic manner, the face of God (and the Church) to people of our time. To enter with 'new eyes' into the Creed, the 'compendium of the Gospel', can greatly assist in the telling about our God and Church in these times characterised by this new evangelisation. We must know who we are before we can speak to others about what we believe is good for all. The place of the Credal section of the CCC indicates as much. It is to be found *before* the sections concerning sacraments, moral and social teaching, and prayer. It makes up 39 per cent[4] of the whole CCC (185-1065).

The Trinity – a simple definition?

The fact that over fifty thousand people in Ireland bought the CCC on its publication shows that we expect something from the Church that will make a difference in our lives and thought.[5] We know from Augustine's celebrated comment that our hearts are restless and will find their rest only in God. The whole Creed speaks of God (199). By definition we can tell others that we believe in God the Father, Son and Holy Spirit. Yet, some years ago, Karl Rahner prompted much reflection when he claimed that in many ways the God we profess to believe in is, in fact, often perceived as a one-person God. Perhaps to exaggerate the impact of his point, Rahner also maintained that if, by some strange hypothesis, we were to say the doctrine of the Trinity were false, little would change in theological and catechetical literature.[6] Catherine LaCugna echoes this concern.[7]

There is a kind of 'exile' of the Trinity in our everyday lives of faith and reflection on what our faith means, an 'Islamicisation' of our faith.

The doctrine of the Trinity is, however, beginning to be rediscovered as being full of personal, social and ecclesial implications.[8] Vatican II contributed greatly in this regard. The CCC is an expression of Vatican II,[9] which Paul VI often called the 'great catechism' of modern times and which, in its ecclesiology, emphasised the Trinity.[10] It is a sign of the times, therefore, that one of the major achievements of the Credal section of the CCC is the consistent presentation of the *trinitarian* structure of our faith.

The Trinity, the life of God – project for humanity
Let's try to tie down a little more what has been said so far. The point is that, unless we really enter into the revelation of God and God's love as God has revealed it, and which is summarised in the Creed, we risk living and presenting a caricature of God and of the Church.

This can be seen on two levels, personal and social. On a personal level, just think of the images we sometimes discover working, even subtly, within us. 'If I am good and do what God tells me, he will reward me, otherwise he will punish me.' This attitude does not speak of the human maturity (27, 144, 307, 355, 374-9),[11] willed by the God who created us out of love (1, 315, 355-379), and brought us back to unity with him and with one another (599-628, 651-655) when we had destroyed things (396-412), and who continues to draw the good out of the bad in all things for those who love him (227, 313, 395, 731-741). The Christian God in whom Catholics believe is not some kind of sadist who says, 'Do penance, have a hard life, obey me and my arbitrary laws, and I will be pleased and reward you.'

Equally untrue is the assertion that the God we believe in is a paternalistic god alien to our responsible autonomy (302, 307, 1036) and keeping us in childish subjection. Here the form of our thinking might run: 'What matters is that I have never done any harm to anyone.... I live my private life, you live yours and, anyway, God would never want to harm us.' If obedience to God were to be seen in these terms, then we would never really understand our relationship with God. God is the Father, the 'You' who addresses me (203), giving me the chance to love him, Infinite Love, and, at the same time, giving me the chance to love every other man, woman and child put next to me in life as a gift. He pours out a unique love upon every person on earth. In establishing a universal communion where we are to be brothers and sisters to one another (337-349, 355-379, 953), he has called us to build together with him a world of reciprocal love, peace and happiness.

At the social level, who we say God is and who we are in relationship to God in Jesus Christ is all-important. It is only in deepening our knowledge of the life of God as a communion of tri-personal love that we can learn how to shape our own social co-existence. To give a 'soul' to society, we need to go to the *trinitarian* foundations of what the Church proposes in its teaching[12] in areas such as economy and work (307, 378, 531, 544, 853, 899), the inter-relationship between groups and cultures (57, 360, 401, 791, 843, 856), questions of social and moral ethics, law and justice (37, 122, 225, 295, 301, 306, 396, 459, 577, 581-2, 782), health issues (159, 364, 988-1014), the concerns of social harmony and art (339, 341, 344, 374-379, 775, 813), the domain of school and education (426-427, 561), social communication (906), politics and public administration (407).

From the Creed to life

There is a world of discoveries to be made in each element of our profession of faith. But while the Creed itself is the point of unity for the whole catechism, we might ask whether there is some kind of prism through which to view the torrent of its articles. At first sight, it appears that the CCC fails to provide one. However, an expression from Vatican II indicates such a prism, namely, the 'hierarchy of truths'.[13] What is not intended is that some truths are more indispensable than others which can be left on the periphery. The notion of a hierarchy of truths means that if we want to understand, for instance, how the world was created, how original sin and redemption are linked, what the life of grace is, the mystery of the Church and the sacraments, the relation between our bodies and life after death, or the Church's social and moral teaching, we have to have eyes which see them in the light of the Trinity and the Incarnation. The Creed is a symphony of doctrines growing from the central themes of Trinity and Incarnation.[14] Two citations from the CCC demonstrate how the 'hierarchy of truths' is indeed the prism through which to read the rest.

> The Paschal Mystery of Christ's cross and Resurrection stands at the centre of the Good News that the apostles, and the Church following them, are to proclaim to the world. God's saving plan was accomplished 'once for all' (*Heb 9:26*) by the redemptive death of his Son Jesus Christ. (571)

What this tells us is that the Christian faith is not a conglomeration of many things, but a living person: Jesus Christ. But this emphasis on the centrality of the life, death and resurrection of Jesus Christ as the centre of the Gospel is linked to another key statement in the CCC:

The mystery of the Most Holy Trinity is the central mystery of Christian faith and life. It is the mystery of God in himself. It is therefore the source of all the other mysteries of faith, the light that enlightens them. It is the most fundamental and essential teaching in the 'hierarchy of the truths of faith' (*GCD* 43) (234).[15]

In other words, our profession of faith is in God as a communion of love between the Father, Son and Holy Spirit revealed in the paschal mystery of Jesus' death and resurrection. Everything else is linked to this. Every element draws upon Jesus Christ who expresses humanly the divine ways of the Trinity (470). And since we are created in God's image, the divine ways expressed in Jesus' life, death and resurrection are the truest ways of being human. Four keys should be kept in mind when reading the Credal section of the CCC. They can be regarded as four aspects of God's art of loving which we too are called to share in and imitate. From the 'compendium of the Gospel', we discover these four keys for 'trinitarian' living (249-260).

1. **God takes the *initiative* in loving us.** The whole Creed tells of God's many and ever-present initiatives as seen in creation (279-379), the fall (385-412), redemption (571-664), the continuing work of Christ and the Holy Spirit in the Church, in the world and in our own personal and social lives (683-987), until the final transformation of the world (988-1065). All life – past, present and future – comes from God as gift. In deepening our knowledge of the Creed we deepen our knowledge of both why and how we ourselves can be and are called to be the first to love, taking the initiative to 'give' in every situation. Nothing from the past, present or future need block this basic dynamism in human being. Perfect love casts out every fear (*1 Jn 4:18*).

2. **God loves us '*as*' himself.** The doctrine of the Triune life of God speaks of the perfect love between the three divine persons. We could say that none of the divine persons is turned in on himself but that each is totally projected in love towards the 'other' (255). The Creed, which summarises the history of salvation, tells God's story of making himself one with us in our history. Such is the love of God that he is totally 'projected' towards us.

In coming among us, Jesus Christ lives our human condition in all its aspects (including all that separates us from God and one another) in such solidarity with us that he could say, in our name, from the cross: 'My God, my God, why have you forsaken me?' (603). Reconciling our being sinfully turned in on ourselves, when Christ is glorified he communicates his glory, the Holy Spirit, to us (690). United to Christ, we too can live totally projected towards God the Father.

Deepening our knowledge of the Creed under this aspect enables us to discover why, how and to what measure we are called to love (459, 735). If Jesus has loved us 'as' himself, we too are to make ourselves one with our neighbour, making our own their sorrows and joys. We are to 'love' our neighbour, each neighbour placed beside us by God. Love one another 'as' I have loved you (*Jn 13:34; 15:12-13*); love your neighbour 'as' yourself (*Gal 5:14*).

3. **God's love is *universal*.** It excludes no one (543, 604-5). God wants to reach out concretely to the whole of humankind (758-776) and bring everyone into the unity of the Trinity (260). He has his way of reaching out to everyone. On the one hand, in Jesus Christ a share in the paschal mystery has been offered to everyone (618). On the other hand, foreshadowed from the world's beginning (760), the Church was established by Jesus Christ as his instrument of unity in the world (775). As the sacrament of the mission of Christ and the Holy Spirit (738), the Church announces, bears, witnesses, makes present and spreads the mystery of the communion of the Trinity (738). The Church herself is modelled on the communion of the divine persons (877). It is in this light that the CCC speaks of both 'Marian' and 'Petrine' dimensions of the Church, the universal sacrament of salvation (770-776).

What emerges from a study of the Credal section of the CCC is a deeper realisation of the 'how' of God's universal love. It indicates that we too must love everyone, believing in God's universal love for all, living and dead. God's 'how' is the Church's 'how'. This also highlights how a collective or communitarian spirituality belongs to the very nature of the Christian vocation. We believe in love (*1 Jn 4:16*). Love hopes all things (*1 Cor 13:7*), and so, wherever we are in the world, we are of the same mind, having the same love (*Phil 2:2*).

4. **God *sees Jesus Christ* in us.** A true understanding of what Jesus Christ has brought about leads us to realise that we have been made share in his relationship with God the Father and the Holy Spirit (654-655, 690). We have been brought into an 'adventure' with God, who has not left us orphans but has, rather, brought us to co-operate with his continuing creative and redeeming work in the world (306-308, 690, 970). We can find a presence of Jesus Christ in every neighbour (544, 598, 678) and, accordingly, in the words of St John of the Cross, at the end of life, we shall be judged on our love (1022). In the time which continues to

the end of the world, doing the will of God is not something negative to be endured in resignation but actively to be sought as our greatest fulfilment (260, 1050). Jesus himself says: 'Those who love me will keep my word, and my Father will love them, and we will come to them and make our home with them' (*Jn 14:23*).

Take one example: God almighty!

Irish people sometimes season their conversation with expressions like 'God almighty!' Since this reference to a divine attribute is found in the very first sentence of the Creed, it is a good example to take by way of indicating just how much is to be found in the Credal statements. The opening sentence of the Creed affirms that we 'believe in God, the Father almighty, creator of heaven and earth'. Commentary in the CCC on this one sentence is distributed over seven paragraphs, taking each of these words one by one because each word has a deep meaning.

In approaching our belief in the 'almighty' God (268-274), the seemingly irreconcilable enigma of suffering and the existence of evil appear. On the one hand, within each of us can be the question: 'If God is almighty, why does he not stop so many terrible world disasters, wars, famines…?' On the other hand, God's omnipotence is also an attribute which threatens many people existentially today. This manifests itself in Ireland, not so much as a theoretical rejection of an omnipotent God as a practical problem with the 'external' authority of the Church: 'Is my freedom or quality of life-style not threatened in some way?'

If we are faithful to the prism through which to view the CCC, we know that we must approach this divine attribute in the light of the Incarnation and Trinity. The history of salvation, which reaches a high point in Jesus Christ, shows us a God who bears all things, endures all things, hopes all things, precisely because God is the almighty one of love, 'right to the end'. In the divine life, love never comes to an end in giving the 'other' space and freedom. The Paschal Mystery of Jesus' life, death and resurrection reveals the great measure of God's measureless love. This is not an arbitrary, unjust or strange power.

Only faith can discern this power of love when it is made perfect in weakness. It is true that 'faith in God the Father almighty can be put to the test by the experience of evil and suffering. God can sometimes seem to be absent and incapable of stopping evil' (272). But the New Testament is full of the paradox of good and evil, of power and weakness. In later sections the CCC itself outlines how the omnipotent God comes to meet us and give himself to us, to the point of Jesus' total humiliation on the cross where he gives everything.

In relating our consideration of the divine attribute of omnipotence to Jesus, we begin to understand and are not scandalised by the apparent impotence of God. It is the impotence of the Almighty One who knows how to create out of nothing, bring order out of chaos, open a new realm of Spirit-filled light in the midst of darkness. Only faith can really recognise the omnipotence of God in this reality. The CCC indicates a model to us: *the* woman of the Gospel, Mary. In her 'yes' nothing is impossible to God and so she sings: 'The Almighty has done great things for me; holy is his name' (273). Hers is the full understanding of omnipotence (484-502, 721-726, 963-972).

It is this picture of co-operation with God's omnipotence which indicates that our dependence on a source beyond ourselves can be life-giving and not threatening. Through the Church God wants to communicate a life-project which sets us free. God has given us life and brings that life ahead, not in opposition to us but in a mysterious, providential project with us. Earthenware vessels carry great treasures (*2 Cor 4:7*).

The Creed today

The common language of faith provided by the Creed isn't just about words. Likewise, the doctrinal section of the Catechism is certainly not meant to be a dry book containing a whole series of propositions in which we believe and to which we adhere. In this regard, St Thomas Aquinas, the great thirteenth-century theologian, says that the believer's act of faith does not stop in what is enunciated, that is, in the concept studied, but reaches the reality (170). In other words, when I believe a truth I am not reaching an abstract doctrine but reaching God, touching God.

The early Christian community gathered in the name of Jesus and, in experiencing the presence of their glorious Lord, acclaimed him. Their acclamations were the origins of the articles of the Creed. It is up to us to allow that unity with God and one another to be reconstituted as the background which allows the Word of God to be told and acclaimed again in our day. Otherwise our Christianity risks becoming a museum-piece or an array of neon signs without the electricity. Going back to the train journey I mentioned at the beginning, it was in telling my philosopher-companion about my own rediscovery of God as Love that our journey was shortened.

FOR DISCUSSION AND REFLECTION
1. What does the Creed tell you about God (a) when things are going well? (b) when things are not going so well?

2. What do you understand of your relationship with each of the Three Persons of God – Father, Son and Holy Spirit?

3. Jesus has revealed that God is a 'family-community' of love between Father, Son and Holy Spirit. How does this understanding of God help you to live out your faith as a member of a Christian family at home, at work, or in the parish?

FURTHER READING
1. The Irish Theological Commission, *A New Age of the Spirit: A Catholic Response to the New Age Phenomenon* (Dublin: Veritas, 1994).
2. Catherine Mowry LaCugna, 'The Trinitarian Mystery of God', in Francis Schüssler Fiorenza and John P. Galvin (eds.), *Systematic Theology: Roman Catholic Perspectives* (Dublin: Gill & Macmillan, 1992, pp. 149-192).
3. Hans Urs Von Balthasar, *Credo: Meditations on the Apostles' Creed* (Edinburgh: T. & T. Clark, 1990).

5

THE SEVEN SACRAMENTS OF THE CHURCH

Catherine Gorman

Entitled 'The Celebration of the Christian Mystery', the second part of the CCC deals with liturgy, and is divided into two major sections which are preceded by nine introductory paragraphs. The CCC progresses from fundamental questions concerning 'liturgy', through a presentation of the various aspects involved in Christian liturgy, to an exposition of each of the seven sacramental rites as they are celebrated today.

Such an approach has much to offer any programme of liturgical catechesis, the provision of which is called for (1075), and is urgently needed in Ireland today. Coming thirty-one years after *Sacrosanctum concilium*, what does the CCC offer those of us interested in promoting liturgical catechesis in Ireland, as we approach the next millenium? Firstly, four of the issues raised in the introductory paragraphs are relevant to the general situation in Ireland today *vis-à-vis* liturgy. Secondly, in the section entitled 'The Sacramental Economy', there is a good exposition of general liturgical principles which often remain unattended to when it comes to liturgical celebration. Thirdly, the CCC's presentation of the seven sacraments in Section Two offers us the opportunity to review both our present celebration of these rites, and the theology we express through such celebration.

Introductory paragraphs

The *first* question that is raised in these introductory paragraphs is 'Why liturgy?' It echoes the question of many in Ireland today who are asking themselves 'What's the point? Why am I still going?' In answering, the CCC reminds us that liturgy is our proclamation of the life, death, resurrection, ascension and final coming of Jesus Christ, *and* of our relationship with him. That is all that any liturgy is about – a retelling and proclaiming of the Paschal Mystery, of what God has done for us in Christ. To put it another way, we could describe liturgy in terms of the words of the Magnificat: liturgy is our way of saying that the Lord has done great things for us, Holy is God's name.

The *second* important question these introductory paragraphs ask is: 'What does the word liturgy mean?' We are told that the Greek word *lei-*

tourgia was a term which described a 'public work' or 'service' which involved people (1069). In the Christian tradition, liturgy means 'the participation of the People of God in the work of God'. That is it in a nutshell. 'Liturgy' speaks of our participation in and celebration of our relationship with God; our proclamation of the Good News of what God has done for us; our willingness to be of service to others. The CCC reminds us that in the New Testament, the term 'liturgy' has a wider application than today, for in the early Church 'liturgy' referred not only to worship but also to works of charity (1070).

The *third* important point to be raised in this Introduction is that 'Liturgy must be preceded by evangelisation, faith and conversion' (1072). This stands to reason from what has been said in the earlier paragraphs – if Christian liturgy is about proclaiming and participating in the Paschal Mystery of Christ, then liturgy presumes that some form of evangelisation has already taken place; it presumes some faith commitment to Christ, and at least a basic conversion to the person of Christ, on the part of the person participating. With such a basis as our context for liturgy, then we gather together because we want to express certain truths that are important to us, namely: that Christ is risen from the dead and that, through baptism, we share his risen life; that even if we can't make sense of life from time to time, we believe that God is good and we come to liturgy to find nourishment for our faith; that we are a community which gathers week in, week out, supporting each other on our individual life-journeys.

The *fourth* point to be highlighted from this Introduction is the acknowledgement of the diversity of the Church's rites and cultures (1075). This paragraph goes on to repeat the call made elsewhere in the CCC for regional catechisms which would concretise and localise what is presented here as universal and fundamental. There is much in these introductory paragraphs to provide a model for such local programmes in Ireland today.

Section One – The Sacramental Economy

Sacramental economy refers to the way in which we play our part in God's plan for us, through our participation in the Sacraments. We can do this because of what Christ has done for us, in his life, death, resurrection, ascension and final coming, that is, through his Paschal Mystery.

Chapter One – The Paschal Mystery in the Age of the Church

This chapter looks at liturgy as the work of the Trinity (article 1), and at the Paschal Mystery in the Church's sacraments (article 2).

How is liturgy the work of the Trinity? Here we are introduced to the liturgical concept of *anamnesis* or remembering (1103). The action of remembering in liturgy has richer connotations than are normally associated with remembering in day-to-day living. Most of the time we use the words 'remember' or 'memorial' in reference to something that is in the past, ended, finished. In liturgy our remembering makes Christ present to us; he is in our midst. It is the Spirit who enables us to remember what Christ did, the Spirit who was Christ's gift to the Church. The liturgy is seen as the work of the Trinity in that it is through the Spirit that we remember what Christ did, and in remembering that we make present and join with Christ in his offering of himself to the Father. All Christian liturgy is essentially trinitarian – it is made in the name of the God Jesus revealed, the Father, Son and Spirit. The clearest example of this is perhaps in the Eucharistic Prayer, when we pray to the Father, through the Son, in the power of the Spirit.

From this trinitarian context the second article in chapter one focuses more specifically on a theology of the sacraments (1113-1134). The teaching of the Council of Trent, that the sacraments were instituted by Christ, is reiterated and supported by quoting St Leo's phrase that what was visible in Christ's earthly life is now passed over into the sacraments (1114-5). The sacraments presuppose faith *and* they also nourish, strengthen and express our faith (1123). The sacraments are efficacious and confer grace because, first and foremost, they are the actions of Christ (1127). It is Christ himself who acts in the sacraments to communicate with the participant. The sacrament 'is not wrought by the righteousness of either the celebrant or the recipient, but by the power of God'. The term *ex opere operato* means that the sacraments are primarily the work of Christ. 'From the moment a sacrament is celebrated in accordance with the intention of the Church, the power of Christ and his Spirit acts in and through it, independently of the personal holiness of the minister. Nevertheless the fruits of the sacrament also depend on the disposition of the one who receives them' (1128). This statement reflects well the dynamism of the relationship between the minister, the participant, and the power of God.

Chapter Two – *The sacramental celebration of the Paschal Mystery*
In chapter two we have a very fine introduction to liturgy in terms of both its structure and content. This chapter uses the question-and-answer method people expect to find in a catechism, and in a relatively small number of paragraphs – fifty-one in all – the basic principles of Christian liturgy are offered in a clear and informative manner.

The answer to the question *'Who celebrates?'* is 'all the baptised'. The

CCC quotes paragraph 14 of the *Constitution on the Sacred Liturgy* where it states that the 'Church earnestly desires that all the faithful be led to that full, conscious, and active participation in liturgical celebrations, called for by the very nature of the liturgy. Such participation by the Christian people as a ' "chosen race, a royal priesthood, a holy nation" (*1 Pet 2:9*), is their right and duty by reason of their baptism' (1141).

Under the question *'How is the Liturgy Celebrated?'* there are some very fine paragraphs on sign and symbol, which include some important points on the place of the Word in liturgy, on actions and gestures, on singing and music, and on the role and function of holy images in our liturgy. In this way, the CCC reminds us that liturgy engages all our human senses. What we see, hear, touch, taste and smell enables us to enter into the sacred mystery that is at the heart of liturgy.

Addressing the question: *'When is the Liturgy Celebrated?'* we have again a fine basis from which to understand the why and wherefore of the liturgical year. Under the same question, the Liturgy of the Hours, or as it is still popularly called, the Divine Office, is spoken of and we are reminded of the intimate relationship that exists between the celebration of Eucharist and the celebration of Morning Prayer, Evening Prayer and the other smaller hours of prayer (1174). The Liturgy of the Hours is described as an extension of the Eucharistic celebration which does not exclude but calls forth in a complementary way the various devotions of the People of God, especially adoration and worship of the Blessed Sacrament (1178). In making this point, and in quoting in full the recommendation from *Sacrosanctum concilium* which urges the reintroduction of at least Evening Prayer on Sundays and feasts (1175), there is a challenge to the present status quo in many parishes.

Finally, in dealing with the question *'Where is the Liturgy Celebrated?'* the CCC begins by quoting John 4:25 where we hear Jesus being asked about the true place of worship. He responds that true worship is worship in spirit and in truth. We are reminded that the whole earth is sacred and that the faithful, the people who gather, are the living stones of God's temple (1179). From this context the CCC goes on to speak of points to be remembered when constructing places for worship. This broader canvas of seeing *all* ground, so to speak, as holy ground, and the restating of the original meaning of the word 'Church' to describe the people who gather rather than the place of gathering, are two very basic issues which we have still not fully grasped.

This chapter also devotes ten paragraphs (1200-1209) to the various liturgical traditions within the Christian Church. These highlight the different ways in which Christian faith can be expressed. This point is developed further in section two, by referring to the Eastern Church's way of celebrating the sacraments while presenting the sacramental rites familiar to Roman Catholics. Such a presentation broadens our vision of how Christian liturgy is celebrated, and that can only be to the good.

Section Two – The Seven Sacraments of the Church

This section begins by introducing the seven sacraments as touching all stages of human life and presents the way it will speak of the seven, in terms of three groupings:
1. The sacraments of initiation – Baptism, Confirmation and Eucharist;
2. The sacraments of healing – Reconciliation, Anointing;
3. The sacraments at the service of community – Orders and Matrimony.

In this the CCC implicitly reminds us that the sacraments are not so much isolated moments or events but expressions of what it means to live a Christian life. While some of us, for various reasons, may not participate in all seven sacraments, nevertheless each sacrament speaks to every individual who has committed him/herself to following Christ. In other words, what is at the heart of each sacrament is the Christian vision of life which is applicable to us all.

Chapter One – The sacraments of Christian initiation

1. **Baptism** (1213-1284). In presenting Baptism the CCC begins by looking at what the word baptism means – an immersing or plunging into water. In quoting Romans 6:3 in full, it reminds us of how the early Church saw this 'drowning' in water: 'Did you not know that when you entered the waters of baptism, you entered the tomb with Christ, so as to rise with him to newness of life.' Reinforcing the fact that Baptism is an Easter event, the CCC then presents the text of the blessing of the baptismal water, used at the Easter Vigil. This central belief of Baptism – that when we are baptised we enter into Christ's death and resurrection – is fundamental to a true understanding of this rite.

In the baptism of children the praying of the Our Father around the altar table during the Rite of Baptism expresses the link between Baptism and Eucharist (1244). The newly baptised will make their own way to the altar table at first Communion time, a fulfilment of all that is begun in Baptism. Some of our parish celebrations of infant baptism focus on the central areas around which this rite is celebrated: beginning at the door of the Church with the joyful greeting, then processing to listen to God's Word proclaimed at the ambo, moving to the font for the immersion and, finally, gathering around the altar table to pray as Jesus taught us, and to invoke God's blessing on those with direct responsibility for the newly-baptised child. In highlighting this movement to the altar table (1244) the CCC is challenging the rest of us to look at our pastoral practice and to review such practice in terms of what the ritual is expressing.

In stating how Baptism is celebrated the CCC outlines how we initiate adults and children in the West and it also presents the practice which obtains in the East, where children receive Baptism, Confirmation and Eucharist during the one rite. A good summary of these two traditions is found in paragraphs 1229-1233. We are given an account of the gratuitous nature of salvation in infant baptism (1250). We are also informed of the necessity of Baptism, when we are told that 'God has bound salvation to the sacrament of Baptism. But God himself is not bound by the sacraments' (1257). The two principal effects of Baptism are stated as 'purification from sins and new birth in the Holy Spirit' (1262). The baptised person is 'a new creature', a 'temple of the Holy Spirit' (1265-6). Through Baptism people are incorporated 'into the Church', The Body of Christ (1267-70).

2. **Confirmation** (1285-1321). In speaking of Confirmation as 'the full outpouring of the Holy Spirit' (1302), the CCC presents the different celebrations of this rite in the Christian Churches of the East and West. The Eastern Church has one main form of initiation (1292), during which the candidate is baptised, anointed ('confirmed') and receives first Eucharist. In the Western Church, there are two main forms of initiation. The initiation of children involves three separate rites, extending from infancy to teenage years, whereas the Rite of Christian Initiation of Adults (RCIA), reintroduced by Vatican II, involves one rite in which Baptism, Anointing and first Eucharist are celebrated together.

While the practice in the Eastern Church gives greater emphasis to the unitary nature of the initiation rite, the Western rituals express the communion of the individual with the bishop and with the wider Church. In the West the intimate connection of Confirmation with Baptism and Eucharist is expressed in the renewing of baptismal vows as part of the Confirmation Rite and in celebrating Confirmation in the context of Eucharist. Preparation for Confirmation is primarily aimed at awakening 'a sense of belonging to the Church of Jesus Christ' (1309). The CCC stresses the relationship between Confirmation and Baptism by encouraging the same sponsor or godparent for both (1311).

The order in which these sacraments are spoken of throughout these articles and in the next article on Eucharist is: Baptism, Confirmation,

Eucharist. Though this is obviously *not* the typical order in which we celebrate them in the West, when it comes to the initiation of children, such a presentation of these sacraments will surely support the ongoing theological and pastoral reflection in the Western Churches concerning the order in which we celebrate Confirmation and first Eucharist.

3. Eucharist (1322-1419). This section begins by identifying the various terms associated with the Eucharist and giving a short explanation of each one. In exploring these familiar terms ('Mass', 'Sacrifice', 'Eucharist', etc.) with groups over the years, I have found that knowing the original meanings always provokes great interest and a richer grasp of what is central to this sacrament. These paragraphs (1328-1332) offer essential material for study and reflection to all who participate in Eucharist.

Under the title 'The Eucharist in the Economy of Salvation' (1333-1344), the reality of bread and wine throughout Jewish history and in Christ's earthly ministry is presented. In taking, blessing and breaking the sacred bread, in pouring the consecrated wine, Eucharist challenges us to see the sacred in the ordinary. It is through the ordinary stuff of life – in this case, food and drink – that God meets us. There is a fine exposition of the various parts of the Mass and their meaning (1345-1355), as well as a good account of the various ways in which Christ is present during Mass (1373-77).

There is a quote from St Augustine's sermon regarding the implications of receiving the Body and Blood of Christ in Communion, and the Church being the Body of Christ in the world today. 'To that which you are you respond "Amen" and by responding to it you assent to it. For you hear the words, "the Body of Christ" and respond "Amen". Be then a member of the Body of Christ that your *Amen* may be true' (1396). This is a powerful, challenging text, and its theology is echoed in paragraph 1397, which reminds us that our celebration of Eucharist commits us to the poor. There is a description of the Eucharist as it is celebrated in the different Christian Churches (1398-1401), and a reminder that our earthly celebration of Eucharist is a foretaste of the eternal banquet. There is much in this article on Eucharist that needs to be made available to all who eat the Bread, drink the Cup and proclaim Christ's death and resurrection until he comes again in glory.

Chapter Two - the sacraments of healing

1. Penance and Reconciliation (1422-1498). That this sacrament is given such a title is to be warmly welcomed. The popular name,

'Confession', refers to only one element of this rite. In contrast, calling it 'Reconciliation' offers a fuller description of what we celebrate. Of the various dimensions of the sacrament, namely, contrition, confession, penance, forgiveness and reconciliation, the element that is often perceived as the most difficult for many is the confession of sin. The CCC reminds us that the act of confession is not solely a confession of our sins but also a confession of our faith in God, that is, we confess both who we are *and* who God is for us. The relationship between Baptism and Reconciliation (1425-6) is well captured in the quote from St Ambrose who spoke of Reconciliation as a second Baptism, a baptism of tears (1429).

After an outline of the history of this ritual (1447) we have the Church's present teaching on the celebration of this sacrament (1457); all who have attained the age of reason are bound to confess serious sin once a year; anyone committing mortal sin must confess before receiving Communion; children must celebrate this sacrament before first Communion. We are reminded that the Penance received is to correspond with the nature of the sin and to take account of the personal situation of the penitent (1460). There are grave sins which incur excommunication (1463). In danger of death any priest, even if deprived of faculties for hearing confession, can absolve from excommunication. After a reference to indulgences (1471-79) there is an outline of the various forms and rites of the sacrament today (1480-84).

2. **Anointing of the Sick** (1499-1532). The second sacrament of healing is the Anointing of the Sick. The opening paragraphs in the CCC on this sacrament remind us both of Christ's compassion for the sick and of his identifying with them. It quotes Matthew 25:36: 'I was sick and you visited me' (1503), and also the passage in James 5:14-15 which is seen as the basis of this sacramental rite (1510).

There follows a broad outline of the history of anointing, reminding us that over the centuries anointing was conferred more and more on those who were dying (1512). In effect, that is how the name Extreme Unction (oil used at the extremity of life) arose. This sacrament is available to those who are ill, to the elderly, to those undergoing an operation, and its celebration can be repeated if necessary (1514-15). Ideally it should be a communal celebration involving family and friends (1517). In terms of the effects of the sacrament the CCC speaks of the gift of the Spirit, of our union with Christ in his passion and, in the case of the dying, a preparation for the final stages of one's earthly life (1520-1523). The relationship of Reconciliation, Anointing and Eucharist at the end of our earthly Christian existence is paralleled with Baptism (Reconciliation being a second baptism), Confirmation (anointing with the Spirit) and Eucharist, which begins our Christian journey – which is a very beautiful way of seeing these moments at the beginning and end of our earthly Christian lives (1525).

Chapter Three – The sacraments at the service of communion
Grounding these two sacraments in Baptism, Confirmation and Eucharist, the CCC speaks of both Orders and Matrimony as being directed primarily towards *others* rather than towards the ordained and the couple exclusively (1534). It goes on to state that these sacraments confer a particular mission in the Church and serve to build up the People of God (1535).

1. **Holy Orders** (1536-1600). We are told (1536) that the institution of Orders is dealt with in the section on the Creed in Part One. Then we learn why the sacrament is called Orders (1537-8) and we are reminded that in the early Church other groups were given the appellation 'Orders', for example catechumens and widows. Today the term is limited to degrees within the ordained priesthood.

The CCC reiterates the relationship between the priesthood of the baptised and the priesthood of the ordained within the one priesthood of Christ (1546 and 1547). Christ is the one true priest mediator between God and God's people, in whose priesthood we have been called to share by virtue of Baptism. Through Baptism each one is called to continue Christ's ministry in the world today. The ministerial hierarchical priesthood of the ordained is at the service of the common priesthood of the baptised.

The third section of this article deals with the degrees within the ordained priesthood, that of bishop, priest and deacon. After a mention of the reintroduction of the Order of Permanent Deacons (1571), the text speaks of celibacy as practised in the Western Church and also presents the Eastern practice where married men are ordained as priests (1579-80). Finally, the effects of the sacrament of Orders are stated, with reference to some of the prayer texts of the rites, where the essence of a spirituality for the ordained priesthood is also to be found.

2. **Matrimony** (1601-1666). The context in which the CCC speaks of marriage is that of covenanted love. The well-being of both partners in this covenant is the focus of the sacrament. In placing the primary emphasis on the loving commitment of the partners, out of which chil-

dren may be born, the CCC will support catechetical efforts to correct the common, stereotypical perception of Church teaching on marriage, where the primary emphasis is seen to be the procreation of children. The CCC emphasises the equality of men and women (1604-5). Much work will need to be done in local catechisms so that the kernel truth presented here concerning the equality and mutuality of woman and man will be recognised as Church teaching.

In the opening section on marriage in God's plan, there are three paragraphs entitled 'Virginity for the Sake of the Kingdom' (1618-20). Here it is stated that our understanding of Christian marriage is inseparable from an understanding of the consecrated life exemplified by those men and women who commit themselves to Christ in what we commonly call 'religious life'. While the CCC states that these two ways of life 'reinforce each other' (1620), further work is needed in local catechisms to recognise the complementarity of these vocations in today's society.

Under the heading 'Matrimonial Consent' (1632), the CCC supports the well-established pre-marriage courses, stating that preparation for marriage is of prime importance, so that such consent is made freely and responsibly. The indissolubility of marriage is spoken of (1640, 1644). In 'The Domestic Church' we hear that the family is the first and primary school of faith (1655-58). This again has implications for local catechisms and catechetical programmes, so that the family's capacity to worship in the home can be nurtured, and their participation in local parish structures can be facilitated.

One final paragraph in this article speaks of the single life. More needs to be said in local catechisms, so that we can have a richer image of the many ways in which adults live out the one baptismal faith which we all share.

Other liturgical celebrations

The final chapter of Section Two is divided into two articles, one dealing with sacramentals, the other with Christian funerals. The first of these articles reminds us of the sacramentality of all life, a vision of existence which is rooted in our baptism. 'Sacramentals derive from the baptismal priesthood: every baptised person is called to be a "blessing", and to bless' (1669). Such an understanding of ourselves can only enhance our participation in the sacred rites of our Church. The second article, on Christian funerals, highlights some of the moments of the rites surrounding death and refers to the revised *Order of Christian Funerals* published in 1992.

Conclusion

In summary, I think two points need to be made in regard to the CCC, Part Two. *Firstly,* our understanding of sacraments needs to be rooted in a sacramental vision of life that sees the sacred in the ordinary, that sees Baptism as our call to be beloved – the beloved son or daughter of God. In this vision of life, the beloved who sees God in all things, becomes the servant and lives a life modelled on the life of Christ who saw the good in all.

Secondly, much of Part Two of the CCC presents the basic teaching concerning Christian liturgy which is still unfamiliar to many baptised adults in Ireland. A resource text for adult catechesis and religious education, based on the material presented here, would be an invaluable contribution to the catechetical work in liturgy which is still to be done in the Irish Catholic Church.

FOR DISCUSSION AND REFLECTION
1. What is the relationship between private prayer, communal services (para-liturgies), and the sacraments?
2. Evaluate your parish's celebration of the sacraments.
3. How can the positive yet still unfamiliar Church teaching on liturgy become more widely known and experienced in your parish?

FURTHER READING
1. Monika Hellwig, *The Meaning of the Sacraments* (Ohio: Pflaum Press, 1981).
2. Lawrence Mick, *Understanding the Sacraments Today* (Collegeville, Minnesota: The Liturgical Press, 1987).
3. Seán Swayne (ed.) *The Sacraments: A Pastoral Directory* (Dublin: Veritas, 1976).

6

HOW DO YOU KNOW
WHAT IS RIGHT OR WRONG?
Morality and the Catechism

Donal Harrington

Where have the ten commandments gone?
The moral section of the CCC (1691-2557) can be viewed through the lens of two of the most frequently expressed contemporary sentiments about morality. One of these asks: 'Where have the ten commandments gone? Why are they not being taught in school? Is there no right and wrong anymore?' The other says: 'It is very hard to know what is right and what is wrong any more – if you do what you feel is right, then you are right.'

Both of these sentiments deserve to be looked at sympathetically and critically. The first, which is voiced mainly by an older generation, is admirable in its desire for order in society and for standards in moral education. On the other hand, its tone can suggest the wish for an authoritarian kind of morality which has had its day. Nevertheless, in a time of deep moral confusion it is understandable that people would pine for the clarity of an age that is gone.

The second sentiment, voiced mainly by young adults, is to be cherished for the value it puts on freedom and the dignity of the individual conscience – the very casualties of an authoritarian morality. However, its tone suggests a subjectivism of the weakest kind, a stance of 'I feel, therefore I'm right'. This stance is clearly false to anybody who has had the experience of discovering, a day or a week later, that they were wrong! But, again, it is understandable; in a time of deep moral confusion it is a way of dealing with the despair generated by the apparently hopeless task of ever finding objectivity in morals.

A cursory glance at the moral section of the CCC reveals that its main content is structured around the ten commandments (2052-2557). This would suggest that the CCC reflects the first of our two sentiments. But it is not quite so simple, because there is more to the understanding of the ten commandments than meets the eye.

Invitation and response

If a group of people were to be asked what the ten commandments are, a probable answer would be that they are guidelines for moral behaviour, given to us by God, articulating basic values and norms, telling us what to do and what to avoid. If I were to mark that answer, I would give it about six out of ten – meaning that it is true as far as it goes, but that it does not go far enough. It would be like asking what *Hamlet* is all about and being told that it is about a murder. Although the answer is true it misses the point.

In fact, the CCC claims far more for the commandments, as can be discerned by listening to the language it uses (2056-2062). It says that they are a 'gift', 'the gift of God himself'. It says that they are 'a path of life', and talks of their 'liberating power'. It says that the commandments 'must first be understood in the context of the Exodus', that they themselves 'come in the second place' and only 'take on their full meaning within the Covenant'. They are about 'the implications of belonging to God'; they present moral existence as 'a *response* to the Lord's loving initiative' (2062).

Of course the commandments *are* guidelines for moral behaviour, but it is clear from the language of paragraph 2062 that this is only the beginning of what the commandments mean for Christians, and that to see them as no more than laws or guidelines would be a failure to see the wood for the trees. That means that we could have an accurate understanding of what the commandments prohibit and of what they enjoin, and yet totally miss their meaning.

The vital words above are the words 'Exodus' and 'Covenant'. They refer to God's liberation of God's people from all bondage, to God's invitation to all God's people to life together. The commandments are about response to this. They are a summary statement of what response is like. Like any response they make no sense in isolation from the invitation. That is why the commandments cannot be understood by going through them one by one. They can be understood only by understanding the invitation.

The section explaining the commandments begins by quoting two classical source texts from Exodus 20 and Deuteronomy 5 alongside each other. Both these presentations begin not with the first commandment, but with the words, 'I am the Lord your God, who brought you out of the land of Egypt, out of the house of bondage'. Then the commandments follow, as a gift from God, revealing the 'how' – how this can be, not just a past event, but a present experience; how God's people can continue to come up out of bondage. It has been said that the commandments are the 'today' of Exodus-Covenant.

There is one very important implication of understanding the commandments in this context. Very often we see morality simply in terms of what we do. We go on to think in 'if… then…' terms, that if I do good then I will be rewarded, I will merit God's love. This is the wrong way to see Christian morality; it amounts to seeing the commandments without the Covenant, not seeing the wood for the trees.

Properly understood, morality begins not with what *we* do, but with what *God* does. In the words of St John, it is not that we loved God, but that God loved us (2083). It is not 'if… then… ' but 'because… therefore… '. Because God has loved us, because God has brought us up out of Egypt, we are liberated to love in return. It is not that I do good and then God will love me. It is that God loves me and therefore I can do good, as a loving response that could not be were it not enabled by the prior invitation and initiative of God.

This issue has been a persistent source of problems with morality in the history of the Church. Jesus himself was faced with the self-sufficient attitude of the Pharisees. St Paul had to contend with the thinking among some of his converts that salvation depended not on God's grace, but on their observance of the law. St Augustine had to deal with the heresy of the Pelagians, that Christ was no more than a good example and that we are perfectly able to achieve moral rectitude unaided.

More recently, the language of 'saving my soul' and of 'earning' or 'meriting' salvation has betrayed the same mentality. We have been guilty of surrendering to the mood of trying frantically to earn God's love, instead of joyfully responding to a love that is simply given. As long as we consider the commandments in isolation from Exodus-Covenant, this heresy will continue to distort our moral consciousness.

A communal response

But there is more to the question: 'What are the commandments?' The first aspect of the answer was to say that they represent a response to God's graceful initiative. A second aspect is their communal setting. When God calls or invites, it is a people that is called rather than individuals. Brought up out of Egypt, Israel is called to be God's people in the world. Of course there are stories of individuals being called or chosen – Samuel, David, the various prophets – but this is secondary. What God is doing is fashioning a people that will be God's own people. The concern of the commandments is not just what you or I do or avoid; it is what we as a people become.

This second aspect of the meaning of the commandments stands as a corrective to our tendency to interpret Christian morality in an individualistic manner. Notwithstanding what truth it contains, the phrase 'saving my soul' captures all that is wrong here. It suggests that being moral is something I do alone, a matter of praying well and not interfering with the life or character or property of others – the negative 'thou shalt not' formulation of the commandments adds to this impression. The ten commandments are not simply about how to be a person; they are about how to be a people, God's people (2077).

Faith and justice

A third aspect of what the commandments are emerges from reflecting on the significance of their division into two groups in the CCC. This is nothing new; it simply takes up Jesus' distillation of the commandments into the two great commandments (2055). Thus, the first three are about love of God (no other gods, respect God's name, keep the sabbath), and the remainder are about love of neighbour (honour one's parents, do not kill or commit adultery or steal or bear false witness or covet what belongs to another).

But, from another angle, this is not so much a dividing into two groups as a bringing together of two concerns, perhaps the two great concerns of the Old Testament. One of these is faith in God, and this includes the monotheism of the people of Israel and the importance they placed on worship of the one true God (2084-86). The other is their concern for right relationships throughout society (1807). And, as in the words of the song, 'you can't have one without the other', it is the refrain of the Old Testament that worship without the practice of justice is false worship.

More recently we have heard the same refrain again. The document from the 1971 Synod of Bishops said that 'action on behalf of justice and participation in the transformation of the world fully appear to us as a constitutive dimension of the preaching of the gospel....' There has been some debate about the word 'constitutive'. Some would prefer to say that action for justice is an 'important' part of faith. But the word 'constitutive' says more; it says that action for justice is intrinsic and essential to faith. Faith impels Christians to realise God's justice in the world, and anything less is less than faith.

This too leads us to question how we understand the ten commandments. It is often noted how good young people are at seeing through hypocrisy and detecting inconsistency. They are alive to the contradiction between the fervent prayer in the church on Sunday and the backbiting and lack of caring of the next six days. In this they are close to the prophets. For both Deuteronomy and Jeremiah, 'listening' was a very important word. Really to listen to the ten commandments would have an effect on one's whole life. To pray would be to listen and to listen would be to care.

Social analysis
A fourth and final aspect of the meaning of the commandments leads directly from this. Because the commandments integrate faith and justice, they can function as a tool or instrument of what is known today as 'social analysis'. Moses says, 'Keep these words that I am commanding you today in your heart... talk about them... Bind them as a sign on your hand... write them on the doorposts of your house and on your gates' (*Deuteronomy 6: 6-9*). If, in the spirit of Moses, we 'internalise' or take to heart the deep meaning of the commandments, we learn to see society through this lens.

This is exactly what the Old Testament prophets were about. Take for instance the stories of David and Bathsheba (*2 Samuel 11-12*) and of Ahab and Naboth (*1 Kings 21*). Bathsheba, the wife of the soldier Uriah, becomes pregnant by King David. David's efforts to cover up his indiscretion lead him eventually to have Uriah put in the front line of battle, so that after he is killed David can marry Bathsheba without anybody being the wiser. In the other story, when Naboth refuses to sell his vineyard to King Ahab, the king's wife Jezebel has a couple of base fellows falsely accuse Naboth of blaspheming, so that after he is executed Ahab can take over the vineyard.

They are both stories of horrific injustice, all the might of the king coming down on an innocent individual so that desire might be satisfied. But how many of the commandments have been broken? Thou shalt not kill; thou shalt not commit adultery; thou shalt not steal; thou shalt not bear false witness; thou shalt not covet thy neighbour's wife; thou shalt not covet thy neighbour's goods. Here, six out of ten is quite impressive!

In fact it is worse, it is nine out of ten! In both stories the prophet appears on the scene, Nathan to David, Elijah to Ahab. In each case the prophet's essential message is; in doing this you have despised the word of the Lord. In other words, in breaking commandment you have broken covenant; in failing your neighbour you have failed the Lord. In breaking the last seven commandments you also break the first three (2069).

The two stories illustrate graphically that the ten commandments are not dry and dusty rules, but go to the heart of what being God's people is all about. We cannot but be affected by the wrongdoing in each story, because the breaking of the commandments goes against everything we believe about life and community and God. To see what is going on in society in terms of the ten commandments is to see very deeply indeed.

The commandments have this same potential today, and this explains the way in which they are presented in the CCC. Together they constitute a frame onto which a wide variety of issues can be 'pegged'. For instance, the first commandment, about not having false gods, is an opportunity for discussing faith and doubt (2087-8), prayer and adoration (2096-8), superstition (2111) and magic (2117). The fourth commandment, about honouring one's parents, is also an opportunity for discussing the duties of parents towards children (2221-30) and of society towards the family (2234-7). The eighth commandment, about not bearing false witness, is an opportunity for discussing truthfulness and witnessing to the truth (2464-74), and discretion (2488-9) and media ethics (2493-9).

Most remarkable in this regard is the presentation of the seventh commandment: 'Thou shalt not steal'. Older catechisms talked of stealing and restitution at a one-to-one level. But the CCC speaks about the Church's right and duty to engage in social and economic issues (2420). It goes on to talk about two Christian ideas that have the power to revolutionise society. One is that the right of all God's people to an adequate share in God's creation is a more fundamental value than the value of private property (2403). The other is that a Christian society is committed to giving preferential attention to people in need (2448). This implies that if wealth is being amassed while human need goes unmet, Covenant is being broken and God's people are not God's people.

The old and the new

Despite the rich potential of the CCC's presentation of the commandments, its failure to present them in the context of the New Testament is most unfortunate. While it does highlight Jesus' distilling of the commandments into the two great commandments, there is a lamentable absence from this section of the CCC of such themes as the call to conversion and discipleship. New Testament morality does not begin by saying, 'I am the Lord your God who brought you out of the land of Egypt.' Its first proclamation is, 'The time is fulfilled and the Kingdom of God has come near; repent and believe in the good news' (*Mark 1:15*).

Part of the problem here lies in the structure of the moral section of the CCC. It is in two parts, the first of which (1699-2029) is a general consideration of morality under such headings as freeedom, human acts, the passions, conscience, sin, the person in society, the moral law, grace and merit; and the second of which (2052-2557) is a treatment of the range of specific moral issues within the framework of the ten commandments. Despite the introduction of some new themes, this is essentially the same structure that was to be found in all textbooks or manuals of moral theology from around the year 1600 right up to the 1950s.

That structure is now obsolete in moral theology, and for a number of reasons – its excessive legalism, its failure to appreciate the subjective dimension of morality, its individualistic understanding of morality, but most of all, the virtual absence of any Christological focus. The books which began to appear in the 1950s had titles such as *The Master Calls, The Primacy of Charity in the Moral Life, The Law of Christ, The Following of Christ*. It is amazing to us that such themes should have been so new, for today they are the basic currency of Christian moral reflection. It is therefore difficult to understand why the Catechism chooses a format that is forty years out of date and recognised to be inadequate.

Morality and subjectivity

I have been responding to the question: 'Where have the ten commandments gone?' by suggesting how we might best read what the CCC has to say about them. That leaves our other question, namely: 'What does the CCC make of the contemporary emphasis on subjectivity in morality?' It is clear about rights and wrongs, about an objective moral order; but what does it say about the individual's own feelings and attitudes, opinions and convictions?'

Morality is within

In fact the CCC says quite an amount on this theme. When presenting the last two commandments ('Thou shalt not covet...'), it remarks: 'The tenth commandment concerns the intentions of the heart; with the ninth it summarises all the precepts of the Law' (2534). This suggests that the commandments happen inside you. It brings to mind the words of Jesus; 'For out of the heart come evil intentions, murder, adultery, fornication, theft, false witness, slander' (*Matthew 15:19*). So the commandments are not a matter of external conformity, but of subjective or interior disposition. They are about feelings and attitudes and values.

Surprisingly, the chapter where the subjective aspect of morality is possibly best represented is that concerning the sixth commandment. While much of the chapter is taken up with a discussion of sins against chastity and marriage (within which there is a disproportionate preoccupation with procreation), the chapter begins with a most positive presentation of the meaning of the virtue of chastity (2337-59).

Many an older book of moral theology gave an impression of chastity as being a matter of putting the lid on one's sexuality. (Because of this connotation, the word 'chastity' may be in need of some better replacement today.) But the CCC speaks quite differently. It speaks of love as the nature of God and the vocation of humanity (2331). It sees sexuality as intimately linked to love (2332-3), to be acknowledged and accepted. Chastity is about the integration of sexuality within the person, which is a 'long and exacting work' of self-mastery, never completed for once and for all, more difficult at some times in life than at others (2342).

The significance of this presentation is that the CCC sees morality as a matter of personal growth (2343) and not just about laws 'out there'. It thinks in terms of the subjective dispositions whereby the person can reach the truly good. It is because it thinks in this way that the Catechism can be alive and sensitive to the difficulties people experience in their reaching for the good.

An example of this sensitivity is the CCC's treatment of homosexuality (2357-2359). It is to be expected that it would speak of homosexual acts as 'intrinsically disordered' (though, oddly, it spoke a few paragraphs earlier of masturbation as 'intrinsically *and gravely* disordered'!). But it also notes that many a homosexual person experiences the condition as a trial, and speaks of how the call to chastity will be realised only gradually. Whatever reservations there may be about the treatment of sexual morality, the point here is the recognition of gradualness or growth in the moral life.

In an earlier section the CCC had spoken about the 'passions', by which it means the feelings that lead to actions. There it said that just because you feel strongly does not mean that you are right (or wrong). Rather, you have to learn to feel strongly about the right things, about love and goodness (1768-1770). Again, the implication is that obeying the commandments is about getting yourself right, inside.

Morality is high achievement

The section on the passions is followed by a consideration of conscience. It is widely perceived today that the Church is not interested in conscience, but only in authority and obedience. There may be some truth in this, but what the CCC says paints another side of the picture. For instance: 'It is important for every person to be sufficiently present to himself in order to hear and follow the voice of his conscience. This requirement of *interiority* is all the more necessary as life often distracts us from any reflection, self-examination or introspection' (1779).

Talk about following one's conscience can be facile, suggesting that it can be done quite readily if only certain authority figures would stop obstructing the way. Passages like this suggest something more realistic, namely, that following one's conscience is a high achievement, demanding self-knowledge and courage. The freedom to do what is good is not something one has but something one acquires; something, indeed, which it is difficult to acquire (1783).

This may be the point at which to consider a point made in the CCC's section on sin. After giving the traditional definition of mortal sin (grave matter, full knowledge, full consent), it continues; '*Unintentional ignorance* can diminish or even remove the imputability of a grave offence.... The promptings of feelings and passions can also diminish the voluntary and free character of an offence, as can external pressures or pathological disorders' (1860).

When morality is seen only in objective terms, we tend to think of the moral agent as being like a computer – press the command, instant response. The force of this passage is its appreciation that we are not moral machines, always acting with 'full knowledge' and 'full consent'. In fact, when we reflect on it, we begin to wonder just how many actions are carried out with such clarity of vision and unambiguity of purpose.

In these various ways, the CCC gives its answer to the contemporary fashion of subjectivism in morals. Essentially these passages convey a sense that the moral subject is far more complex than today's subjectivism and relativism understand. We do not simply act as we feel; we do not simply 'follow our conscience'. There is also the refinement of feeling, the nurturing of inner wisdom, the growth in self-knowledge, the coping with pressures and fears and disorders.

To help and to heal

But for all this the CCC remains unbalanced. It spends a hundred and sixty pages talking about morality, but with only a sentence or paragraph here and there about what it is like subjectively. The ratio is typical of the manual tradition in moral theology. What is needed is another hundred and sixty pages about what is involved in becoming moral.

When a woman who had been sexually abused was asked during a radio interview what damage it had done to her, she said that she was 'incapable of compassion'. We need to realise that when we present the moral ideal, when we say, for instance, 'love one another', more people than we may imagine are whispering in reply, 'I can't'. They are too wounded, too afraid. There are feelings, failures, hurts, unconscious driving forces, mixed motives and external pressures, which can sometimes make it impossible to respond. Few situations will be as heart-rending as that just instanced, but all point to the same conclusion. What many people need in their moral education and formation is not preaching, but healing, not being told what to do, but being helped in the doing of it.

This suggests that there is a dual focus to the Church's moral teaching, one aspect of which sets forth what is right and wrong, while the other enables people in becoming moral. The first focus makes for a prophetic moral voice in a morally confused world where the ten commandments seem to have been forgotten. The other makes for a pastoral moral concern in a world where people suffer and frequently limp rather than stride towards the moral ideal. A poverty with regard to either aspect of the focus is ultimately an impoverishment of both.

FOR DISCUSSION AND REFLECTION
1. What is the difference between saying that morality is about obeying laws and saying that it is about responding to a person?
2. What do people need in order to help them to be moral? Is it preaching, or healing, or something else?
3. It has been said that you could be obeying all the ten commandments and still be totally selfish. How could that statement make sense?
4. Which is more important – the sixth or the seventh commandment?

FURTHER READING
Vincent MacNamara, *The Truth in Love: Reflections on Christian Morality* (Dublin: Gill & Macmillan, 1988).
James Gaffney, *Newness of Life: A Modern Introduction to Catholic Ethics* (New York: Paulist Press, 1979).
Richard Gula, *Reason Informed by Faith: Foundations of Catholic Morality* (New York: Paulist Press, 1989).

7

PRAYER IN THE CATECHISM

Donal Neary SJ

Contemporary developments in prayer life
The past thirty years in Ireland and elsewhere have shown a marked interest in personal prayer. Movements such as the Charismatic Renewal, directed retreats, Exercises in Daily Life, Síol, prayer groups, scripture groups, schools of meditation, as well as the inner-directed movements of the other schools of meditation and what is generally called 'The New Age', have blossomed and reached many people. What people expect from prayer and how they pray has changed.

Traditional forms of personal prayer such as the Rosary, the Stations of the Cross, and others have lessened in impact and popularity. At times there are questions about the vagueness of prayer, and about how central Jesus Christ is to personal prayer. Paradoxically, in a time when faith and the practice of faith have weakened, an interest in prayer has developed in certain pockets of the Church. This new interest is centred on personal experience. Various methods and schools of prayer aim at developing a friend-to-friend relationship with God, sometimes centred on Jesus Christ. A movement into silent prayer and the prayer of the mantra has also developed.

New dynamics in prayer are largely centred on the encouragement of a personal relationship with God which is honest, authentic and sincere. While a former type of prayer was centred on Christ – like praying the Rosary or the Stations of the Cross – it was more centred on the *content* of the prayer than on the *person* praying. Many of the developments in prayer at present encourage sharing honestly with God how we feel, expressing anger to God, even anger at God, discerning in prayer God's call and God's will in our lives. Prayer is now seen more as a relationship; with an equal stress on the one praying and on the one we pray to (2558). The CCC accepts that new direction and also gives a beautiful treatment of the place of Jesus in prayer (2599-2616).

Sharing prayer in groups, availing of spiritual direction, and taking part in meditation groups all reveal the role of community within prayer. There has been a renewal of the belief that none of us prays on our own, even if we pray alone, and that our prayer can grow with the aid of prayer guides or spiritual directors.

A positive element has been the rediscovery of the image of a loving God, who loves each of us as a son or daughter (2567). This unique loving relationship grounds an acceptance of each person as he or she is, with each of us journeying our *unique* way to God. This was well summed up by St Ignatius in a letter to Francis Borgia, and quoted by J. Veale: 'God sees what is best for each one. And knowing all things he shows each one the road to take and helps with grace to follow it. But we may need time before discovering, perhaps by trial and error, our own special way to God, the surest and happiest for a person in this life'.[1] Put another way, it echoes the well-tried advice of Cassian: 'Pray as you can, not as you can't.'

The contribution of the CCC (2558-2864)
The fourth part of the CCC has been called the best part; this may be because its theme is non-controversial, or because it also reflects an acceptance of many trends in prayer today. As well as offering a perspective on some contemporary developments in prayer (2689-91), it also provides a systematic analysis of the text of 'the fundamental Christian prayer' (2759), the 'Our Father'.[2] Other encouraging and helpful insights into the life of prayer can be found, especially in the following areas: placing the initiative for prayer with God (2559-61); assessing the fruits of prayer in how we live our lives in love (2658); rooting Christian prayer in Jesus (2598); and offering some answers to the question 'How do Christians pray?' (2759).

Initiative of God
Prayer is firstly the action of God: We may forget or hide from the Creator '...yet the living and true God tirelessly invites each person to that mysterious encounter known as prayer. In prayer the faithful God's initiative of love always comes first; our own first step is always a response' (2567). God is the beginner and the teacher of prayer. Prayer is relaxing into the mystery of being loved, called and chosen by God in Jesus Christ (2564). There are echoes here of the poem 'A Giving', by Irish poet Brendan Kennelly:

> I give thanks
> To...
> The reticent God who goes about his work
> Determined to hold on to nothing....
> I listen to the sound of doors
> Opening and closing in the street.

They are like the heartbeats of this creator
Who gives everything away.
I do not understand
Such constant evacuation of the heart...
I grasp a little of the giving
And hold it close as my own flesh.
It is this little
That I give to you.[3]

Love as the fruit of prayer

In the Christian tradition, the Church's prayer is 'founded on the apostolic faith, *authenticated by charity* (my emphasis); nourished in the Eucharist' (2624). Thus, the great test of Christian prayer is charity: not how sweet your mantra nor how vivid your imagination, not how fragrant your incense and ecological your prayer place, but how you live your life. Faith introduces us to charity, and one feeds the other; both are nourished by the community in the Eucharist. This vision addresses the problem of the vagueness that may be found in some treatments and practices of prayer.

The love of God is where prayer begins; love is the summit of prayer. Prayer is in the service of love; this is a particularly Christian view of prayer. It is not an activity of itself. Christian prayer is judged by its fruits of a more loving, compassionate life geared towards service.

The ordinary and prayer

The ordinary is the place of prayer. One person, talking of prayer, says that: 'I can always pray because I can always thank God for something in my busy day.' People who swear at God for the hardships of life, someone at odds with God because of the relationship which broke up, someone thankful for love or help... all these experiences are openings and invitations to prayer. There is a clear echo here of the contemporary desire to link prayer explicitly with the ordinary 'events of *each day*' (2659).

The CCC puts it very well: 'Prayer in the events of each day and each moment is one of the secrets of the kingdom revealed to "little children", to the servants of Christ, to the poor of the Beatitudes. It is right and good to pray so that the coming of the Kingdom of justice and peace may influence the march of history, but it is just as important to bring the help of prayer into humble, everyday situations; all forms of prayer can be the leaven to which the Lord compares the Kingdom' (2660).

Forms and traditions of prayer

Five forms of prayer are integral to the public prayer of the Church and probably contain most of the movements of personal prayer: adoration, petition, intercession, thanksgiving and praise (2626-43). Catechists will find here a valuable help for teaching prayer, especially to the young and to children.

Traditions of prayer, as taught by the great teachers of prayer, bear witness 'to the integration of the faith into a particular human environment and its history' (2684). Once again, this links prayer with the concerns of the Church and of the world. For example, one might hope that the thirst for justice – among people and for the earth – may be creative of a new spirituality and forms of prayer, just as former ages gave rise to their own brands of spirituality and of prayer.

'Servants of prayer' (2685-90) is a strange phrase. It refers, in fact, to teachers of prayer: the family, ordained ministers, religious, catechists, prayer groups and spiritual directors. Places 'favourable' for prayer also have their importance (2691). These are very important paragraphs: they reflect the experience of all of us who try to pray. We are formed in prayer by people and groups who pray; the prayer of the liturgy is a teacher of prayer, not from its documents, but from its people (2655). The importance of spiritual direction and prayer groups has been a marked innovation in the development of prayer in recent years. The CCC welcomes these new developments (2689-90) and encourages them.

The prayer of Jesus (2599-2616)

Jesus is presented as the source and goal of a Christian's prayer. This is the CCC at its best! Jesus teaches his apostles to pray by inviting them to pray with him (2620-21). Have you ever been with someone who is praying? You can learn to pray by being in the presence of a praying person. Similarly with Jesus. The apostles often watched him praying; maybe they listened to him when he prayed aloud, and they certainly would have seen him at prayer in the synagogue. For the prayer of Jesus was personal, communal and rooted both in life and in the tradition of his own faith community (2599). He brought people with him and they were jolted into questions by his praying. Often the teacher – or a priest at Mass – is asked: 'How do you pray?' 'Don't talk to me of prayer', they say: 'Show me. Don't preach about it, tell me how you do it or don't do it. Don't just write about it, but write about it as it can be done'.

Jesus learned to pray from within his tradition; he also learned something new about prayer: it is filial (2599). Jesus' filial prayer is the prayer of the Son watching and waiting for his Father, and doing what his Father wants. His prayer is the gift of himself to the Father; the self-giving of the Trinity, as on the cross (2746-48). He gives up his voice, his life, his spirit. Jesus' prayer has all the hallmarks of a deeply loving relationship; it is like 'friend talking to friend', just as Moses spoke with God.

Jesus prayed at decisive moments (2601), as he did before choosing the Twelve and before the Passion. We find in our own experience that crisis-experiences and decision-times are gateways to prayer and an experience of the Transcendent.

Jesus prayed in solitude (2602). One of today's difficulties with prayer is the difficulty of attaining solitude. Just to be alone without the distractions of the TV, the personal stereo or the daily paper is a difficulty. Just to be at ease in one's own company can be too lonely and thus a block to prayer. But solitude is a pillar of prayer.

And Jesus' prayer was inclusive of all people (2602). The CCC presents the Last Supper prayer as a summing-up of all of Jesus' prayer. He draws us within that prayer, praying 'not only for these, but for all who will believe through them'. It is the prayer of the unity of all creation.[4]

Jesus began all prayer with thanksgiving (2604), as in some examples from the gospel.[5] Thanksgiving is a pillar of prayer (2637-8). It is the gold in the middle of prayer and the enlivening of the memory. Jesus seems to have been a very grateful person. The examen prayer of St Ignatius is very much a model of Jesus' prayer. Thanksgiving, discernment and self-giving are parts of the Ignatian prayer which is recommended daily to people. Sorrow for sin is how our prayer differs from the prayer of Jesus (2631).

And why do we pray? As Pope John Paul writes, 'to fulfil your ministry'.[6] The ministries of teaching, parenting, preaching and suffering are all made full in prayer. Prayer, in the CCC, is always for love. It will not always be peaceful, but will often involve a struggle (2725). It is in the service of love. It is to fulfil the work of God. Does this mean that prayer is an end in itself? No; but there is emptiness in the life that is not prayed. We will notice a quality of fulness in the life of the person who prays – mother, father, teacher – as we notice a quality in the lives of those who have deep friendships or love good music. It is an integration, a deeper love and a willingness to be reconciled (2608).

Prayer of petition (2734-2741)

The CCC gives a lot of attention to the prayer of petition (2629-36). Rightly. It is a major question of prayer – Why is my prayer not heard? Why did God not cure a little child? Why did peace in Northern Ireland take twenty-five years of prayer? Did God not want it?

All prayer, while not always answered, is heard. None is wasted. We get something different from what we ask for. In all prayer the heart is transformed (2739). The prayer of petition in Luke 11 ends up with the promise of the Holy Spirit. All prayers, in fact, are heard and answered, but with the gift of the Holy Spirit (2741). The Holy Spirit can comfort the afflicted and afflict the comfortable. The action of the Holy Spirit is not always peaceful. People may pray for success in business; possibly a lack of success may open their hearts to the poor.

In proposing reasons why we might not be heard, the CCC seems unequal to the task (2736-7): 'Because we do not know how to pray. Because we do not ask according to the will of God. Because we ask with a divided heart'. We seem to be rebuked here by the CCC for praying for anything specific. Endean, quoting Thomas Aquinas, writes : 'We pray in order that our asking bring about those things which God has determined would be obtained only through our prayers'.[7] Thomas respects here the desires of the person and the mystery of God. His point of view is summed up in Endean's commentary: 'Indeed God does not need to be told what we need, but we need to remind ourselves of our dependence on divine help. Indeed, we cannot change God's mind, but there are some realities which God has willed to bring about only by means of our prayer'.[8] Jesus also seems to recommend us to ask heartily, with urgency and boldness, and to know that at the end the Father gives the Holy Spirit.

Missing links

In this very positive and encouraging approach to prayer, some areas are given less than adequate attention. These are, firstly, the link between the human and the spiritual aspects of a person's life; secondly, the question of discernment; and, thirdly, the work of creative adaptation.

The human and the spiritual

What does the CCC say about ordinary difficulties in prayer? Things like, 'I get bored at prayer, nothing happens, I don't feel God's presence'. Maybe the CCC is more geared to the quiet monk than the busy business person, to the contemplative nun than the harassed mother, to the well-to-do than the poor, to the western Christian than the African or Indian.

The difficulties described are distraction (2729), dryness (2731), lack of faith (2732) and 'depression due to lax ascetical practice' (2733). The treatment of difficulties is weak and somewhat discouraging of the efforts of good people in prayer. There is a lack of attention to the effects on prayer of poor self-esteem, irrational guilt and shame. We might look for some reference to the links between people's personal difficulties and their prayer, but we do not find such links, which have figured prominently in the literature of prayer of the past thirty years, as for example, in the popular books of William Barry, Anthony de Mello and Sheila Cassidy.

For many active people, difficulties in prayer spring not from great sinfulness or oddity, but from normal human needs for affection, affirmation, and/or because of self-abasement, anger, perfectionism, guilt and self-hatred. Conflict in life shows itself in prayer: the CCC doesn't hint at this universal aspect of spiritual growth. Difficulties of dryness have more to do with the darkness of self-hatred than with theology; difficulties of not finding time for prayer have as much to do with poor self-esteem and guilt as with a busy schedule, and boredom at prayer has as much to do with boredom with myself as boredom with God.

Dryness can be a gift of God. Difficulties in prayer are not just the person's fault. For most people they are the stuff of life and prayer mingled together. There is a lack of distinction in the CCC between dryness and darkness,[9] as mentioned above, with little attention given to the influences of real depression on prayer, or to the gifts of God in the difficulties of prayer.[10] It would be tempting to try to replace the passage about the battle 'against our dullness and laziness' (2742), with something like this: 'against our dullness and laziness, *our wounds carried from the history of our backgrounds and our many faults not of our own making, against the weakness of the human being which is handed on from the wounded history of parents and others*, the battle of prayer is that of humble, trusting, persevering and transforming love.'

Discernment

The rediscovery of the language of relationship as the language of prayer and faith will raise questions about the use of battle terminology (2725). Any relationship – human or divine – presented in battle[11] terminology would be suspect. I wonder does the CCC take this new shift – from prayer as struggle to prayer as relationship (and struggle in the context of relationship) – seriously enough? Had the chapter been better discerned, would the language, sadly so sexist, be different? For the theme of discernment is missing also. Little attention is given to the ways of sifting various moods, feelings, intuitions and calls in prayer and discovering God's call and God's will in life. Prayer and the life of love are intimately connected, but *the dynamic of this link is discernment*.

Descriptive, not definitive

The CCC is best read as a *description* of prayer; and it is not definitive. Would an Indian write it differently? Or an Irish woman? Would a woman of any race rewrite it? Probably. Endean writes: 'This section of the Catechism is best taken as giving us, simply, a list of themes that should be borne in mind when catechesis on prayer is being planned... the individual catechist should precisely not repeat what is said in the text but rather take it as a basis on which to make responsible variations. What the text provides is a starting point for creativity and discernment'.[12] One is reminded here of the words of the prologue: 'By design, this Catechism does not set out to provide the adaptations of doctrinal presentations and catechetical methods required by the differences of culture, age, spiritual maturity, and social and ecclesial condition among all those to whom it is addressed. Such indispensable adaptations are the responsibility of particular catechisms and, even more, of those who instruct the faithful' (24).

Its descriptive, rather than definitive nature is well caught in a comment of J. Veale on Ignatius of Loyola: 'If Ignatius had had the word "mystical" to use, I am fairly sure he would have refused to use it. Even more, if he had been challenged to say, "Come now, do you mean mystical in the strict sense, or the broad sense? Are you talking about acquired or infused, ordinary or extraordinary?" He would have kept his counsel. He would say that it is enough to know how to respond... that there is a great spectrum of degrees of unitive grace.'[13]

Prayer brings us into the deepest mysteries of life: of self and of God, of the relationship between God and his people, of the deepest mysteries of human life like desire and sin, love and emptiness. The CCC encourages us to pray and to look for the changes that only prayer can bring: the transformation of the heart in love. This is what prayer is about, and this is also what makes for human happiness and fulfilment. The questions posed by the CCC are only marks on paper if they do not invite each of us into the mystery of prayer, into the life of God who thirsts for us as we thirst for God (2560): 'If you knew the gift of God, and who it is that is saying to you, "Give me a drink," you would have asked him, and he would have given you living water; everyone who drinks of this water will be thirsty again, but those who drink of the water that I will give them will never be thirsty. The water that I will give will become in them a spring of water gushing up to eternal life.'[14]

FOR DISCUSSION AND REFLECTION
1. Which questions about prayer from your experience of Christian life does the CCC deal with?
2. Are there any questions on prayer which you had hoped the CCC would deal with and which you find are omitted?
3. Christian prayer is centred on Christ and modelled on Christ. How does the CCC deal with this aspect of Christian prayer? What difference does it make to prayer when prayer is with or to Christ?

FURTHER READING
Due to the large variety of books on prayer, authors rather than titles are suggested for further reading. The following develop some of the themes of this chapter:
    William A. Barry
    Sheila Cassidy
    Lawrence Freeman
    Michael Paul Gallagher
    John Main
    Ronald Rolheiser
    Anne Thurston

Practical methods and exercises for prayer may be found in books by:
    Anthony de Mello
    Donal Neary

SIGNPOSTS
Finding One's Way in the Catechism

Bishop Donal Murray

The Pope's introduction
The first item in the CCC is the Pope's own introduction – the Apostolic Constitution *Fidei depositum*. This outlines

> how the CCC is related to the Second Vatican Council,
> the process by which it was prepared,
> the way in which the material is arranged
> and the importance and value of the text.

Table of contents
After the Apostolic Constitution and the Prologue which speaks of its structure and purpose, the CCC is divided into four parts. (The subheadings given here are not exactly as in the CCC – they simply summarise the content of each section):

1. *The Profession of Faith*
   The human search for God and God's approach to humanity
   Revelation and Faith
   The Twelve Articles of the Apostles' Creed

2. *The Celebration of the Christian Mystery*
   The Paschal Mystery and the Liturgy
   The Sacraments of Initiation (Baptism, Confirmation, Eucharist)
   The Sacraments of Healing (Reconciliation and Anointing)
   The Sacraments at the Service of Communion (Orders and Marriage)
   Other Liturgical Celebrations.

3. *Life in Christ*
   Human Dignity
   The Human Community
   God's Salvation
   The Ten Commandments

4. *Christian Prayer*
   The Call to Prayer
   The Tradition of Prayer
   The Life of Prayer (Forms of Prayer, The Battle of Prayer, Prayer of Jesus)
   Commentary on the Lord's Prayer

It is worth reading the full Table of Contents several times until you are familiar with the general shape of the Catechism. It is also worth returning to it from time to time in order to keep the overall picture in mind.

Subject Index

The Subject Index is introduced by a note which says that it aims to give 'the most comprehensive survey possible of the contents, not the most complete listing of all references to a given subject'. References which are of very minor significance may be omitted.

References are given by paragraph rather than page number. Each paragraph is numbered – from 1 to 2865. [The numbering in the text does not stand out as clearly as one might have wished.] The main subject headings are in **bold print** with sub-headings in ordinary print; references to 'In Brief' sections are in *italics*. At the end of major subject headings there are cross-references to other related subject headings.

The cover

The logo on the front cover is based on a pagan motif adapted by the early Christians. It 'suggests certain characteristics of this Catechism: Christ, the Good Shepherd who leads and protects his faithful (the lamb) by his authority (the staff) draws them by the melodious symphony of the truth (the panpipes) and makes them lie down in the shade of the "tree of life", his redeeming Cross which opens paradise'.

Look at the pictures

Most important among the illustrations are the four at the beginning of each of the four parts. The technicalities of printing and binding have resulted in the positioning of these pieces several pages away from the opening page of the part so that their introductory character may easily be missed. They are intended to set the tone or the spirit and to relate the subject matter to Christ:

1. A third-century fresco showing Jesus, Son of Mary as the long awaited Messiah introduces the first section on the profession of faith.

2. A fourth-century fresco depicting Jesus healing the woman with a haemorrhage, introduces the sacraments as 'powers that go forth' from the Body of Christ to heal the wounds of sin and give us new life.

3. A fourth-century carving shows Christ in glory giving the scrolls of the new law to Peter and Paul at the beginning of the section on Life in Christ.

4. The section on prayer is introduced by an eleventh-century miniature showing Christ in prayer to his Father while the disciples look on.

Other illustrations are examples of the variety of artistic representations of Christ or of the Madonna and Child taken from various parts of the English-speaking world. They include a window by Evie Hone depicting the Beatitudes.

The print
In order to indicate the greater or lesser importance of various paragraphs, the CCC uses different print styles.

The use of smaller print indicates that the passage is supplementary or apologetic – that it is in some way a digression from the main thrust of the argument. Many quotations are also given in smaller print; some of these are very useful catechetical resources.

At the end of each section there is a series of brief statements of one or two sentences which summarise what has gone before. These are written in italics, under the heading 'In Brief'. Some of these might usefully be memorised; they could also provide a useful way to sum up and to focus what has been learned in an accurate formula.

Eyes right; eyes left
Because the faith is an organic whole, what is said in any area of the Catechism has to be seen in the light of all the rest. In the margins of each paragraph are cross-references which are well worth pursuing. These are not exhaustive; not all linkages are indicated. The cross-references should not be confused with the paragraph numbers which are not in the margins but indented at the beginning of the first sentence of the paragraph.

Eyes down
The footnotes can be a useful indicator. There are many quotations,

especially from scripture, which someone studying a particular point could profitably follow up – both to see the context of quotations given in the text and to read in full passages which are merely indicated by references.

It is good to note the variety of sources used – not just scripture, the Fathers of the Church and documents of the *magisterium*, but saints and spiritual writers, men and women, down the ages.

Check the sources
There is a detailed index of sources under various headings
- Sacred Scripture
- Professions of Faith
- Ecumenical Councils
- Particular Councils and Synods
- Pontifical Documents
- Canon Law
- Liturgy
- Ecclesiastical Writers

It may sometimes be useful to begin, for instance, with a particular scripture text and to follow up the places in which it occurs, or one might look at the places in which a particular saint is quoted.

You might begin with a document dealing with a topic in which you are interested and see how it is used. [This may yield unexpected results: two of the four references to *Christifideles laici* lead back to a paragraph on canonisation!]

Go to the back of the book
The back cover of the English edition gives a quotation from the Apostolic Constitution in which Pope John Paul outlines the purposes he hopes the Catechism will serve:

1. A sure reference point for teaching Catholic doctrine.

2. An assistance to all the faithful who wish to deepen their knowledge.

3. A support for ecumenical efforts by showing the content and harmony of the Catholic faith.

4. Something which is offered to all those who wish to know what the Catholic Church believes.

Remember the message

In reading nearly seven hundred pages of text, do not forget what it is all about: it is about the life and message of Jesus Christ and the love of the Triune God. The deepest truths about God and about humanity should give rise to reverence and prayer: 'In reading *The Catechism of the Catholic Church* we can perceive the wonderful unity of the mystery of God, his saving will, as well as the central place of Jesus Christ, the only begotten Son of God, sent by the Father, made man in the womb of the Virgin Mary by the power of the Holy Spirit, to be our Saviour. Having died and risen, Christ is always present in his Church, especially in the sacraments; he is the source of our faith, the model of Christian conduct and the Teacher of our prayer' (*Fidei depositum*).

NOTES

Chapter 1: Why a Catechism?
1. This will be referred to throughout this volume as CCC. References to paragraphs of the CCC will be given in parenthesis, e.g. (24).
2. An example familiar to many Irish people would be *A Catechism of Catholic Doctrine,* approved by the Archbishops and Bishops of Ireland, 1951.
3. FD is the Apostolic Constitution, *Fidei depositum,* which launched the CCC.
4. In the French edition of the CCC the four illustrations are correctly situated immediately before the relevant sections. Not so, unfortunately, in the English translation.
5. See the English translation of the Roman Catechism (entitled *Catechism of the Council of Trent for Parish Priests*) translated by McHugh and Callan, and published by Wagner, New York, 1923, pp.1-10.
6. The English translation of *Directorium Catechisticum Generale,* approved by the Sacred Congregation of the Clergy, Rome, 1971. It will be referred to as the GCD.
7. Already there is talk of rewriting the section on capital punishment (2265) to take account of the stronger language of the more recent Papal Encyclical, *Evangelium vitae.*
8. See United States Catholic Conference, *Sharing the Light of Faith,* Washington, 1979.

Chapter 2: Scripture in the Catechism
1. Cf. R. Virgoulay, 'Un texte à références. Ecriture et conciles dans le Catéchisme', *Lumière et Vie,* 216 (1994) 47-59, especially 49-51.
2. Cf. *The Interpretation of the Bible in the Church. Address of His Holiness Pope John Paul II and Document of the Pontifical Biblical Commission* (Rome: Vatican Press, 1993) p. 113; cf. p. 80.
3. For a description and evaluation of this method see *The Interpretation of the Bible in the Church,* pp. 34-41 (cf Note 2).
4. See *The Interpretation of the Bible in the Church,* pp. 44-46 (cf Note 2). This document assures us that 'the usefulness of narrative analysis for the exegesis of the Bible is clear'; ibid. p. 46.
5. See also paragraphs 134 and 1093-1094.
6. *The Interpretation of the Bible in the Church,* p. 50 (cf Note 2).
7. See also *Dei verbum* 8 and *The Interpretation of the Bible in the Church,* p. 85 (cf Note 2).

8. See also the formula the *analogy of Scripture* which is used and explained in the *Dossier of Information* which is quoted below at the beginning of Part II of this chapter.
9. Cf. also paragraph 702: '... when the Church reads the Old Testament, she searches there for what the Spirit ... wants to tell us about Christ'; paragraph 2763: 'All the Scriptures – the Law, the Prophets and the Psalms – are fulfilled in Christ'; paragraph 134: 'All Sacred Scripture is but one book, and that one book is Christ, because all divine Scripture speaks of Christ, and all divine Scripture is fulfilled in Christ'; paragraph 65: 'Christ, the Son of God made man, is the Father's one, perfect and unsurpassable Word.' The CCC frequently quotes Lk 24:25-27, 44-46, or individual verses from these passages, to justify the search for references to Christ and to the mysteries of his life, death and resurrection in the Old Testament; cf. e.g., paragraphs 112, 555, 601, 652, 702, 2625, 2763. See also what the CCC (1094-1095) says on 'typology', as well as the statement on the relationship between the Old and the New Testaments in the Document issued in 1985 by the Pontifical Commission for Relations with the Jews; cf. *Documentation Catholique* 82 (1985) pp. 733-738, especially pp. 734-735. The text has been published in English in E. J. Fisher and L. Klenicki (ed.), *In Our Time: The Flowering of Jewish-Catholic Dialogue* (New York: Paulist Press, 1990). This volume was not available to me.
10. See *The Interpretation of the Bible in the Church*, pp. 82-83 (cf Note 2): 'Persuaded that the mystery of Christ offers the key to interpretation of all scripture, ancient exegesis laboured to find a spiritual sense in the minutest details of the biblical text ... modern exegesis cannot ascribe true interpretative value to this kind of procedure'.
11. See CCC paragraph 121 which asserts that the Books of the Old Testament 'retain a permanent value', and CCC 122 which states that they are 'a storehouse of sublime teaching'. Notice the forceful statement with which paragraph 121 ends: 'The Old Covenant has never been revoked'. This phrase is part of a much-publicised address made by Pope John Paul II at Mainz in Germany in 1980 in the presence of official Jewish representatives. The Pope said: 'The first aspect of this dialogue, namely the meeting between the people of God of the Old Covenant, which has never been revoked by God (cf. Rom 11:29), and the people of God of the New Covenant, is at the same time a dialogue within our Church between the first and second part of its Bible'; cf. N. Lofink, *The Covenant Revoked. Biblical Reflections on Christian-Jewish Dialogue.* Translated by J. J. Scullion (New York: Paulist Press, 1991), p. 5.

12. *The Interpretation of the Bible in the Church*, p. 81(cf Note 2).
13. Ibid., p. 80. See also p. 82: 'the spiritual sense can never be stripped of its connection with the literal sense'.
14. Cf. ibid., p. 82.
15. Cf. 'Le Catéchisme de l'Église Catholique. Dossier d'information de la Commission d'édition', *Documentation Catholique* 89 (1992) pp. 735-741; the quotation is from p. 739.
16. Cf. O. H. Pesch, 'Der neue 'Weltkatechismus'. Vorstellung und Versuch einer gerechten Würdigung,' *Bibel und Kirche*, 48 (1993), pp. 156-162; the quotation is from p. 158.
17. Cf. R. Brown, *The Gospel According to John* (The Anchor Bible). 2 vols. (London: Chapman, 1971), vol. 1, pp. 178-180.
18. Cf. R. Schnackenburg, *The Gospel According to St John* (Herder's Theological Commentary on the New Testament), 3 vols (New York: Herder and Herder; London: Burns & Oates, 1968, 1980, 1982), vol. 1, pp. 425-428.

Chapter 3: I Believe – We Believe: Faith and Doctrine in the Catechism

1. The significance of Mary as a model of faith is highlighted in the following passage: 'And so the Church venerates in Mary the purest realisation of faith' (149). This theme is echoed in the detailed treatment of the place accorded to Mary the Mother of God in the CCC. See, in particular, paragraphs 144, 494, 506-507, 829, 969, 2617.
2. The CCC does include a number of references to the link between faith and love. See paragraphs 162, 2573 and 2849.
3. For a brief but incisive treatment of this theme, see Karl Rahner, *Encyclopedia of Theology* (London: Burns & Oates, 1975), pp. 496-497. A more detailed exposé of this issue by the same theologian can be found in his *Theological Investigations* (London: Darton, Longman & Todd, 1965), Vol. 1, pp. 296-346.
4. For an introduction to a study of the link between faith and work for social justice, see 'Young adult faith and social justice', in *Faith, Religion and Theology*, Hill, Knitter, Madges (eds.) (Mystic, Connecticut: Twenty-third Publications, 1990), pp. 91-117.
5. The most detailed treatment of the theme of faith development is to be found in the writings of James W. Fowler. For a detailed introduction to this theme and to the writings of Fowler see Jeff Astley, 'Faith Development: An Overview', pp.xvii-xxiii; J. W. Fowler, 'Fowler on Fowler', pp. 1-58 and C. Nelson et al., 'Fowler Evaluated', pp. 59-106, all in *Christian Perspectives on Faith Development*, Jeff Astley, Leslie Francis (eds.) (Leominster: Gracewing, Fowler-Wright Books, 1992).

Chapter 4: The Profession of the Christian Faith: the Creeds

1. Michael Paul Gallagher, 'The New Agenda of Unbelief and Faith', in Dermot Lane (ed.), *Religion and Culture in Dialogue: A Challenge for the Next Millennium* (Dublin: Columba Press, 1993) pp. 133-150.
2. G. K. Chesterton, *Christendom in Dublin* (London: Sheed & Ward, 1932), p. 68.
3. *Gaudium et spes,* 19-21.
4. Christoph Schönborn, 'Major themes and Underlying Principles of the Catechism of the Catholic Church', in Joseph Cardinal Ratzinger and Christoph Schönborn, *Introduction to the Catechism* (San Francisco: Ignatius Press, 1994), pp. 37-97, espec. p. 47.
5. See the address given by Bishop Donal Murray, at the Graduation Ceremony at the Mater Dei Institute of Education, 18 November 1994.
6. Karl Rahner, *The Trinity* (London: Burns & Oates, 1970), espec. pp. 10-15. See John O'Donnell, 'Revelation and Trinity', in *The Mystery of the Triune God* (London: Sheed & Ward, 1988), pp. 17-39.
7. Catherine M. LaCugna, 'Making the Most of Trinity Sunday' *Worship* 60 (1986), pp. 210-24.
8. Bruno Forte, *The Trinity as History* (New York: Alba House, 1989); Mary Ann Fatula, *The Triune God of Christian Faith* (Collegeville, Minnesota: The Liturgical Press, 1990).
9. Pope John Paul II's Apostolic Constitution *Fidei depositum,* promulgating the CCC, was published on 11 October 1992, the thirtieth anniversary of the opening of Vatican II.
10. See Forte, op. cit., pp. 206-219.
11. References to the CCC throughout this chapter are limited to the Credal section.
12. The following references to the CCC are merely a few indications in the Credal section which would then have to be complemented with other CCC references to devlop the trinitarian perspective.
13. See Christoph Schönborn, op. cit., pp. 42 - 49. See also W. Henn, 'The Hierarchy of Truths Twenty Years later', *Theological Studies* 48 (1987), pp. 439-71.
14. See Hans Urs von Balthasar, *The Truth is Symphonic: Aspects of Christian Pluralism* (San Francisco: Ignatius Press, 1987); Karl Rahner, *Foundations of Christian Faith* (London: Darton Longman & Todd, 1978), pp. 382-384.
15. See also *Gaudium et spes,* 22 and 24.

Chapter 7: Prayer in the Catechism

1. J. Veale SJ,' Dominant Orthodoxies' in *Milltown Studies*, 1992.
2. Due to constraints of time during the lecture series on the *Catechism*, treatment of section two of the chapter on prayer 'Our Father' was omitted.
3. B. Kennelly, 'A Giving', in *Collected Poems* (Newcastle: Bloodaxe Books, 1981).
4. An interesting example of the prayer of Jesus is a fantasy prayer exercise: to imagine yourself climbing a mountain and in a secret place coming upon Jesus at prayer. You sit and watch. You sit and listen. You taste and feel his prayer. You hear him praying – the words of offering, of compassion, of intercession. And of praying for you. And then he turns to you, and invites you to sit with him and to look on the world from the mountain and pray with him. You have shared in the prayer of Jesus.
5. cf. Mt 11: 28 and Jn 11: 41-42.
6. *Crossing the Threshold of Hope*, 1994.
7. Philip Endean SJ, 'The Relationship Called Prayer', in Walsh (ed.), *A Commentary on the Catechism of the Catholic Church* (London: Geoffrey Chapman, 1994), p. 402.
8. Idem.
9. Cf William Connolly, 'The Experience of Darkness', in *Review for Religious*, 1980.
10. Endean op. cit. p. 407.
11. It might be noted that the first translation of the text used the word 'struggle' rather than 'battle'. Another place where the original translation might have stayed!
12. Endean, op. cit. p. 399.
13. J Veale, 'Dominant Orthodoxies', *Milltown Studies*, 1992.
14. John 4:11.14.

NOTES ON CONTRIBUTORS

Rev. Patrick M. Devitt EdD: Priest of the Dublin Diocese. Head of the Department of Religious Education in the Mater Dei Institute of Education. Parish Chaplain in North William Street. Secretary of the Irish Episcopal Commission on Catechetics.

Rev. Eoin Cassidy PhD: Priest of the Dublin Diocese. Head of Philosophy Department in the Mater Dei Institute of Education. Parish Chaplain in St John's, Clontarf. Lectures in Philosophy in Queen's University, Belfast.

Rev. Breandán Leahy DD: Priest of the Dublin Diocese. Lecturer in Systematic Theology in Holy Cross College, Clonliffe, and in the Mater Dei Institute of Education.

Ms Catherine Gorman M.Rel.Sc.: Graduate of the Mater Dei Institute of Education and of the Department of Theology at Notre Dame University. Liturgy Coordinator in the Mater Dei Institute. Member of the Irish Episcopal Commission for Liturgy.

Rev. Donal Harrington DD: Priest of the Dublin Diocese. Head of the Moral Theology Department in the Mater Dei Institute of Education. Special Assistant to the Diocesan Committee of Pastoral Development and Renewal.

Rev. Donal Neary SJ: Member of the Jesuit community in Gardiner Street, Dublin. Chaplain to the students of the Mater Dei Institute of Education. Author of numerous works on prayer.

Rev. Michael Maher MSC, PhD: Missioner of the Sacred Heart. Head of the Scripture Department in the Mater Dei Institute of Education. Has specialised in Jewish Studies and has a special interest in Irish spirituality.

Most Rev. Donal Murray DD: Titular Bishop of Glendalough and Auxiliary Bishop of Dublin. In charge of the Episcopal Conference's Council for Culture; Secretariate for Non-Believers; and the Irish Inter-Church Meeting, Department of Theological Questions. Member of the Commission on Catechetics and the Joint Committee on Bio-Ethics.